PRADO
MADRID

Newsweek/GREAT MUSEUMS OF THE WORLD

NEW YORK, N.Y.

**GREAT MUSEUMS
OF THE WORLD**

Editorial Director—Carlo Ludovico Ragghianti

Assistant—Giuliana Nannicini

Translation and Editing—Editors of ARTNEWS

Distributed in the U.S.A. by
W. W. NORTON & COMPANY, INC.
500 Fifth Ave.
New York, New York 10110

PRADO
MADRID

Texts by:

Anna Pallucchini

Carlo Ludovicio Ragghianti

Licia Ragghianti Collobi

Design:

Fiorenzo Giorgi

Published by

NEWSWEEK, INC.
& ARNOLDO MONDADORI EDITORE

7th Printing 1980

ISBN: Clothbound Edition 0-88225-236-4
ISBN: Deluxe Edition 0-88225-211-9

Library of Congress Catalog Card No. 68-20028

THE PRADO MUSEUM

F. J. SÁNCHEZ CANTÓN
Director

Quality rather than quantity is what distinguishes the Prado. There are museums in Europe which have a more complete representation of the various schools: they were formed by specialists and are the product of objective, art-historical criteria. But none of them surpasses the Prado's dazzling accumulation of paintings by masters from the 15th to 18th century.

A few statistics can serve as an introduction to a resume of its history and as an indication of its principal treasures, which include not only paintings but important collections of sculpture, drawings, jewelry of the Renaissance and the Baroque period, tapestries, medallions. etc. — although its paintings are the basis of the Prado's fame.

I

The latest *Catalogue of Paintings,* dated 1963, is the 33rd edition (the first appeared in 1819); it includes 2,164 works. That of *Sculpture* compiled by A. Blanco in 1957 lists 364 pieces. One on *Christian Art* by M. Lorente is being printed; the 120 jewels that constitute the so-called "Treasure of the Dauphin" were catalogued by D. Angulo (2nd edition, 1955). The drawings, approximately 4,000, are still being catalogued, except for the 485 Goyas published separately in 1952.

If the preceding data barely express the riches of the Prado, it will be more helpful perhaps to list some of the paintings of the great masters of Italy, Flanders, Holland, Germany, France and Spain. From Italy, the museum owns an admirable example of each of the following: Fra Angelico, Antonello da Messina and Mantegna: 8 Raphaels, 36 Titians, 13 Veroneses and 25 Tintorettos. Netherlandish painting of the 15th and 16th centuries includes 4 panels by the Master of Flémalle, 8 by van der Weyden, an equal number by Bosch, 4 by Patinir, 15 by Antonis Mor; among 17th century Flemish painters are 86 Rubens, 25 van Dycks, 43 Breughel de Velours, 39 Teniers; of the Germans 4 Dürers, 12 Mengs'; of the French 15 Poussins and 10 Claude Lorrains and, among the greatest painters of Spain: 35 El Grecos, plus two sculptures; 50 Velázquezes, the same number of Riberas, 40 Murillos and 118 Goyas apart from the drawings already mentioned.

Note that these proud statistics include no mention of works by such masters as Botticelli, Giorgione, Correggio, Luini, Andrea del Sarto, Lotto, the Bassani, the Carracci, Reni, Guercino, nor, among Northern artists, Bouts, Petrus Christus, van Orley, Gerard David, Mabuse, Massys, nor, from the 17th century, Rembrandt, van Ostade, Wouwermans, Fyt, Snyders, de Vos, Heda, nor, among Spanish painters, Gallego, Berruguete, Juanes, Morales, Sánchez Coello, Ribalta, Zurbaran, Alonso Cano, Juan Carreño, Claudio Coello, Valdés Leal, Luis Paret, Meléndez, V. Loper, all of whom figure in the Prado's collections.

The luster of most of these names and the quantity of their work owned by the museum gives some idea of its importance even before one knows its history and its significance in the history of art, and even after one has noticed that its collections include few Italian Primitives, 17th-century Dutch portraits and domestic interiors or few paintings of the English school. These are understandable deficiencies when one takes into account the way in which the Prado's basic collection was formed.

II

The history of the founding of the museum is closely linked with that of Spain through the 16th, 17th and 18th centuries, because basically it has been the national gallery of a unified country.

Even though kings from both Castile and Aragon showed a taste for miniatures and for paintings during the Middle Ages, the Prado can rarely exhibit examples from that period. Furthermore, the great unifying queen, Isabella the Catholic, owned numerous panels, of which 50 are still preserved in the Royal Palace of Madrid and the Royal Chapel of Granada, yet the Museum owns none of them. Her successors, from her grandson the Emperor Charles V to Ferdinand VII (who founded the Prado), followed her example in taking Spanish and foreign painters into their service, in commissioning works and in acquiring paintings by contemporary artists as well as earlier ones.

It is amazing to observe the abundance and the high quality of the art that the Spanish kings accumulated in their palaces. Especially notable are the taste and culture revealed by the acquisitions of Philip II and his nephew Philip IV. The former acquired works by Titian, Paolo Veronese, Tintoretto and El Greco, that is to say by the modern, daring painters of the day, and also by Hieronymus Bosch, Patinir, Massys, who were called "the strange ones." Although he was an absolute monarch and Flanders was the principal jewel of his crown, and although he profoundly admired the Ghent altarpiece by the van Eyck brothers, Philip resigned himself to commissioning Michel Coxcie to make a copy for the chapel of the Alcázar.

One of the basic characteristics of the Prado's collection appears here: its legitimacy. Even though proceeding from the royal collection and in spite of prolonged Spanish predominance in Europe, our masterpieces came to Spain by commission, by purchase, by gift or by inheritance.

The tastes of Philip IV, as revealed by his collecting, were no less selective. They were stimulated by the influence, or more precisely the friendship, of Velázquez. His connoisseurship is revealed in his relations with Rubens during the painter's second trip to Castile, and in the purchases he made in Antwerp from Ruben's estate after the artist's death. Further evidence of his interest may be found in the correspondence of the king with his Ambassador to London during the sale of the collections of King Charles I.

But there is a further proof of this predilection for beautiful paintings which is at the same time an eloquent indication of how Philip IV's plan to create a gallery of paintings in Madrid had already begun to take shape before the middle of the 17th century. Almost a century before that there had been talk of locating such a museum in the recently constructed royal palace of the Pardo near Madrid (now the residence of the Chief of State; it was partially destroyed by a fire on March 19, 1604). This early project never materialized, and Philip II gave more than 1,150 paintings to the Royal Monastery of St. Lawrence, the Escorial. Since it was for the most part open to the public and only 30 miles from Madrid, it more than satisfied the demands for study by artists and the curiosity of connoisseurs. Nevertheless the Escorial was insufficient for the extraordinary appetite for art of Philip IV who, according to the Aragonese painter Jusepe Martinez (he probably heard it from Velázquez), "proposed to found a gallery decorated with paintings and to seek out master painters so as to choose among their best pictures"; to which Velázquez replied: "I dare, Sir, to go to Rome and Venice to search for and to buy the best paintings that can be found . . ." He left, and after two long years during which Philip grew very impatient, he returned bringing notable acquisitions, but the museum project was never realized, neither in that century nor in the following one, despite enlightened spirits like the painter Mengs who, in a letter published by the traveler Ponz, expounded the idea of a picture gallery that could be installed in the new royal palace in Madrid — as though this idea had never occurred to anyone before.

As we have seen, the project had long preoccupied the court at Madrid as the collections grew through the centuries. The estimate made of the inventories of the royal palaces by the scholar P. Beroqui is amazing: King Charles II possessed 5,539 paintings at his death on November 1, 1700. These riches were seriously depleted in 1734 when the old Alcazar of Madrid burned; further losses were caused by the Wars of Succession and of Independence, losses for which Philip V and Charles III tried to compensate with new purchases. The latter while still a prince bought a large number of paintings, among them the *Cardinal* by Raphael.

One could say that all 11 Spanish kings who ruled during three centuries had a passion for buying paintings.

It has been proved by historical texts that it was not difficult to obtain permission to study or see the royal collections, but what proves it most of all are the principal schools of painting which flourished in Spain: neither the Toledan nor Valencian school at the end of the 16th and beginning of the 17th centuries could have been formed without knowledge of the paintings acquired for Madrid and the Escorial, nor the Sevillan nor Madrilenian school of the 17th century without a profound knowledge of Venetian and Flemish works on exhibit in the capital.

The credit must be given to the kings: great collectors of admirable paintings.

III

It was to the German painter Anton Raphael Mengs, the principal artist at the court of Charles III (who had inherited the Spanish throne at 43 after a 20 year reign in Naples), that one must attribute the monarch's favorable attitude toward the arts and sciences: he dedicated a building to house the Royal Academy of Noble Arts of San Fernando — to put "under one roof" the collections of arts and objects of the natural sciences; he inaugurated the Botanical Garden in the Prado of the Monastery of San Jeronimo el Real; and ordered the construction of the adjoining museum, a commission given to the Neo-Classical architect Don Juan de Villaneuva, who submitted plans on May 30, 1785. The underlying idea of the building was not understood until 1962 when Prof. Rumeu de Armas published "The Political Testament of the Count of Floridablanca" (the most illustrious Spanish governor of his time) and showed that the building was first destined to accommodate both the fine arts and the natural sciences. But by the end of the 18th century, the construction of the Prado was not much advanced, the delay being caused perhaps in part by the death of Charles III in December, 1788. On the other hand, the project to found a picture gallery began to take life, in theory at any rate, early in the new century.

The proposal presented to the Constituent Assembly by Bertrand Barère on May 26, 1791, for the creation of the Louvre museum helped to stimulate the order given by the Minister Urquijo on September 1, 1800, to bring from Seville to Madrid "paintings by Murillo, a measure conforming to the practice of all the civilized nations of Europe where steps are being taken to establish schools and museums in the seat of the Court." That the project was constantly gaining momentum is proved by the fact that in the order of Godoy, revoking that of Urquijo, a "Museum of the King" is mentioned.

The Napoleonic invasion of Spain with its usurpation of the Spanish throne by Joseph Bonaparte crystallized these diffused projects, and in a decree signed by Urquijo on August 20, 1809, a Museum of Paintings was created in Madrid, assembling works from many public establishments including the royal palaces. By another decree two days later, the Palace of Buenavista was designated as the home of this project (the palace today is part of the Defense Ministry). The "Joseph Museum," as it has been called, barely advanced beyond the project stage, but part of the collection that was confiscated from Godoy was left in Buenavista as well as some paintings from abolished monasteries and convents, but civil wars prevented further realization of the scheme.

Meanwhile, the construction of the Prado continued. In 1806 (the dating is not certain), it seems that work was well advanced. During the occupation of Madrid by the French, the ground floor was utilized for stables (a poet cried: "Its royal salons/ in vile uses were profaned"), and also parts of the gutters were pulled off. All of which explains why, when the Ambassador of Napoleon in Madrid (Conde de la Porest) wrote to Paris mentioning a meeting of the Council of State about the Prado Museum (September 20, 1811), *"un sourire général"* was raised since the Prado was considered unfit for formal use. Nobody then was able to predict its future.

12

IV

The end of the Peninsular War and the return of Ferdinand VII to the throne saw a return to the project of the "intruder King," i.e. the establishment of a national museum for paintings, including those from the suppressed convents in the Buenavista Palace and those in the Academy of Fine Arts. But the idea was never realized because the reopened convents demanded their art back, and the Buenavista Palace required extensive repairs.

The Council of Castile expressed its opinion in favor of a royal project for a museum to be organized in "the famous building which was constructed for this purpose at an expense of many millions . . in the paseo of the Prado." The same year that the king entered Madrid, he dictated an order accepting the proposal of the Council, on December 26, 1814.

The two years which followed Ferdinand VII's wedding (his second marriage) to his niece, the Portuguese Infanta Maria Isabel, on September 29, 1816, until her death on December 26, 1818, were decisive for the restoration and completion of the Prado Museum, thanks to the help of the short-lived queen. An official text in March of the same year, in addition to other evidence, states that Count Floridablanca's idea that "the sciences and the arts united would take on new life" continued to develop, and I can add that during the years 1922–32 a stuffed bird of prey perched in some branches, although very moth-eaten, was still on exhibition in a showcase. But one should note that the public galleries of the Museum exhibited only works of art.

The Prado was inaugurated on November 19, 1819. The installation was limited to the rotunda of the main floor and to lateral wings divided into three halls. Not more than only paintings of living or recently deceased artists were shown: Goya, José Madrazo, etc. All the paintings belonged to the Royal Patrimony, and the directors for the first 20 years were aristocrats. The collection grew rapidly. After two years the 311 works in the first catalogue had swelled to 512 in the second, thanks to the installation of the Italian school in the Great Gallery. After six years the museum had acquired considerable riches, always to the detriment of the royal palaces: the 1828 catalogue numbers 755 paintings. It would be tiresome and not very useful in the present context to continue the numerical list of new acquisitions.

V

An architectural study of the building — a jewel of Spanish Neo-Classic art — has been made in an excellent monograph by F. Chueca (Madrid, 1952). What has been said about the nobility of its lines and proportions is well deserved, but the undeniable aptness of Villanueva's construction as a museum of paintings has not always been recognized: the dimensions of the rooms, the height of the walls, the number and placement of intervals — nothing is overwhelming or overpowering.

One should add (as a traveler from Cadiz, Count de Maule, pointed out around

1806) that it was expected that Villaneuva, "after its conclusion would present to the public plans and designs giving a precise description of such a beautiful work"; but the death of the architect and the turbulent years for Spain which followed perhaps explain the fact that such precious documents have not survived. The Prado Museum has on occasion afforded surprises to those who work there and who know it. Thus in 1930 we "discovered" the magnificent rotunda of the ground floor, a superb piece of architecture then without a comfortable access, which in the 18th century could not have had natural light, yet was nevertheless surely intended to be visited and adorned with works of art since it contains four niches. In addition, during the reconstruction of the rotunda on the main floor in 1964, we found, hidden in the woodwork, a ringlike space around the hemisphere with a heavy stone cornice, on the ringlike vault of the rotunda. The discovery of Villanueva's records might clarify these mysteries.

Another special quality of this beautiful building is the additions made during the 19th and 20th centuries, which fit without violating the whole, to the lasting credit of the architects López Agusdo, Arnal, Grases, F. Arbós, P. de Muguruza, M. Lorente, F. Chueca and J. M. de Muguruza, authors of the complements and additions to the work of Villanueva.

The museum continued to thrive and grow at the expense of the Royal collections until the autumn of 1868 when the triumph of the Revolution nationalized it. For 30 years its directors had continued to amass paintings and the catalogue of 1843, which is the work of Pedro de Madrazo, son of José, who was a director of the museum, includes 1,833 paintings; it was basically the same volume which was re-edited until 1920.

The principal novelty in the life of the museum was the creation on June 7, 1912, of the Board of Patronage, which directs it and which immediately began expanding the building with an addition of 24 rooms completed between 1917 and 1920. Then followed the re-design of the main gallery and the construction of a central staircase in 1923–27. In 1955–56, two new wings with a total of 16 rooms were added; in 1963–64, six more were built; presently work has begun on an extension of equal size.

VI

The essential change caused in the museum when it ceased to depend on the Royal Patrimony (and the collections of the Spanish kings) and became the organism of a Ministry, soon resulted in an additional, satellite museum, "The Trinity," named for the order of the former Madrid convent. Its collection, more piled-up than installed, was composed of paintings from suppressed monasteries and convents. There was little room for these or other additions in the Prado and so the museum soon began to distribute paintings on deposit to provincial museums, universities, official offices, etc. But at the same time paintings of certain periods and schools which had been lacking began to enter the collections, including Spanish panels of the 15th and 16th centuries.

The lack of such works in the royal collections, which was beginning to be remedied with the incorporation of the "Trinity" treasures, has been one of the concerns of the Board of Patronage since its creation; today the Prado possesses a good representation (even though incomplete) of Medieval and Renaissance peninsular art which, though related to the Northern "International Style" and to the Flemish and Italian Renaissance, presents vigorous and original characteristics. Notable examples of 12th century mural paintings are also on show.

After what has been said about the origins of the royal collection, it is hardly necessary to insist on the dazzling richness of the total collection, formed by the Italian paintings (the Venetians in particular), by the Netherlandish school with its Gothic fantasy, the Flanders of Rubens and his followers and the 16th to 18th century Spaniards, from El Greco to Goya.

The Board of Patronage was faced with a total absence of English painting and with a small representation of the 17th century Dutch school, easy to explain by the friction between Spain and both countries due to religious and political questions. As has been said, another area poorly represented in the palace collections and, as a consequence, in the Prado, is Italy prior to Raphael. Although it was not easy to fill these gaps, persistent efforts have provided the Prado with a hall of English portraits and some examples which complement aspects of the Dutch school. Good fortune has also graced the museum with eight early Italian panels.

The Prado with its treasures of amazing quality and quantity, despite certain gaps, constitutes one of the finest collections for the study of the course of European painting; it possesses not only the most beautiful examples of the Venetian School in its triumphal moment with "the poems" of Titian and the most varied collection of the mythological and religious creations of Rubens, but also the strictest lessons of Velázquez' and Ribera's confrontation with reality. And if this were not enough to ensure the glory of the Prado, it embodies the liberating flow away from conventions and formulas seen in the diverse explorations of Bosch, Patinir, El Greco and Goya.

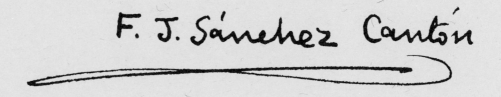

F. J. Sánchez Cantón

ITALY

ANDREA MANTEGNA. *The Death of the Virgin.*

The upper part of this work was mutilated before it reached the Prado. The missing section represented Christ — enclosed in a sort of wrapping of clouds spangled with cherubim against a background of a vault in the architectural style of Alberti — receiving the soul of the Virgin. A fragment has been found in the Vendeghini Collection in Ferrara. Therefore, we can reconstruct the work, aided by the knowledge of a similar iconographic solution in the mosaic of the Mascoli Chapel in St. Mark's, Venice. Various suggestions have been proposed for the relationship between this picture and the mosaic, but critics now believe that the mosaic was a derivation from the Madrid panel, which from its style may be dated around 1460. There is no exact documentation on the work, but it is probable that it was part of the decoration of the chapel in the Castello di S. Giorgio, which Mantegna began for the Gonzaga family around 1459, and which also included the beautiful panels now in the Uffizi. In the 19th century these were reunited to form a triptych, with the *Adoration of the Magi* in the center, and the *Circumcision* and the *Ascension* at the sides. By 1460, Mantegna had completed his youthful Paduan experience and was preparing for his masterpiece in the Camera degli Sposi in Mantua. In our small panel the virtuosity of the epic narrator is transformed into an emotional tension that finds expression in the highly composed structure of the circle of Apostles around the bier (only broken by the figure leaning forward and swinging a thurible over the body of the Virgin), and in the chromatic force of every detail. It was the mellowness of color and perhaps the crystalline luminosity of the landscape elements (a dam on the lake of Mantua?) that suggested Bellini as an author to Adolfo Venturi. This unsustainable hypothesis had a reasonable aspect. It is in the five years between 1456 and 1460 that Bellini was observing Mantegna most attentively, as is proven by his *Transfiguration* in the Museo Correr, which was considered to be by Mantegna.

SANDRO BOTTICELLI. *Nastagio degli Onesti.*   *p. 20*

This illustration of a scene in a Boccaccio story was commissioned for the marriage of Giannozzo Pucci and Lucrezia Bini (1483), as indicated by the coats of arms; stylistic examination confirms this dating. The series of panels is by Botticelli in concept and design, but the execution is mainly studio work and critics recognize in it the collaboration of Bartolomeo di Giovanni. Botticelli had come back from Rome in 1482 famous for the work he had done there and, overloaded with commissions, was obliged to hire assistants. Certainly the drawing is very fine — "all alive with delicate and pungent graces" (Bettini) — and reflects the narrative ability of the master and his penetrating intuition in translating the original novella. In it, Boccaccio tells the tale of an unrequited lover who changes his lady's mind: he made her visualize hell, and the perpetual torment of a cruel woman by the lover who had suffered damnation for her. In the detail reproduced here, the youth is seen pursuing the nude girl; he knocks her to the ground, tears out her heart, throws it to his dogs, then starts the pursuit and torture again, the cycle continuing through eternity. Without question it is the most beautiful of the panels. The space deepens from the shore of Classe to the farther reaches of the marine view; the distant horizon divides the surface into

18

ANDREA MANTEGNA
Isola di Carturo 1431 — Mantua 1506
The Death of the Virgin (ca. 1460)
Panel; 21 1/4″ × 16 1/2″ Provenance: collection of Charles I, King of England.

SANDRO BOTTICELLI
Florence 1445 — Florence 1510
Nastagio degli Onesti (1483)
Detail. Panel; 2'8" × 4'6". One of a series of panels for a nuptial chamber, executed for the marriage of Giannozzo Pucci and Lucrezia Bini (in 1483). With two other episodes, it comes from the Cambó collection in Barcelona.

two areas equal in size and different in intention. And the space is scanned with a certain regularity by the verticals of the pines supporting their green domes. The elegant figures move amid these geometric coordinates, and the fantastic narration is achieved effortlessly in a play of intricate rhythms.

RAPHAEL. *The Madonna of the Fish.*

Nothing is known of how Raphael was commissioned to do this outstanding work. A letter of Summonte, in 1524, indicates that it was then in the chapel of the del Doce or del Duca family in S. Domenico, Naples. It is reasonable to think that it was conceived as an ex-voto for the cure of an eye malady, as is suggested by the presence of Tobias, who is being presented to the Virgin by the Archangel Raphael, and of St. Jerome. Raphael composed the group with a knowledge of curvilinear rhythms that recall the disposition of the figures around the arches in S. Maria della Pace (1514). The figures, however, appear exalted, purified in their reverent approach to the solemn, somewhat cold-looking Virgin, who leaves the principal role to the Child, seen in the act of grasping at the sacred book from which St. Je-

RAPHAEL
Urbino 1482 — Rome 1520
The Madonna of the Fish (ca. 1514)
Canvas (transfered from panel); 7' × 5'2".
Provenance: S. Domenico, Naples, where it remained until 1638; the Duke of Medina, Spanish Viceroy, moved it to Madrid in 1644; the next year it entered the collection of Philip IV.

rome raises his eyes, and leaning affectionately toward the group of the angel and Tobias. The work is not considered to be entirely by the master's hand. Taking into account its less than excellent state of preservation, it is still an outstanding example of the formal and refined "prose" that Raphael knew how to compose during the years in which he created the Stanza of the Fire in the Borgo (1514–16).

RAPHAEL. *Portrait of a Cardinal.*

Masterpiece of Raphael's portrait painting in the first years of his activity in Rome, it is considered contemporary with the Stanza della Segnatura. In particular it is comparable to the fresco of Julius II, in the guise of Gregory IX, approving the decretals delivered to him by St. Raymond of Pennafort — a fresco that cannot be dated after 1511. Raphael's vocation for portraiture was revealed in his earliest work. In the frescoes of the Vatican Stanzas — that poem of human spirituality — numerous portraits of friends and famous personalities of the time appear as historical figures of the past. But despite innumerable suggestions by scholars (the candidates most frequently proposed are Alidosi and Ippolito d'Este), the impenetrable face of this cardinal has managed to maintain its incognito. The impression made by those sealed lips becomes emblematic of the history of this memorable image, which out of its anonymity attains the universality of a human type: the calculating and enigmatic diplomat.

The formal means by which the figure of the cardinal is achieved verges on overstatement. It has been observed that the composition consists of two inverted pyramids joined at their apexes, and shows that play of volumes as perfect forms, almost an obsession in Renaissance painting. And other subtle harmonies have been noted in the play of line that defines the face and the hat. Certainly the impression created of a sense of incorruptible matter — the stuff of which the image is made — emphasizes admirably the inflexible spirituality that must have emanated from the illustrious, aristocratic model.

ANDREA DEL SARTO. *The Sacrifice of Abraham.*   *p. 24*

Vasari relates that Andrea del Sarto, on the suggestion of a Florentine friend who sold art works to Francis I, King of France, made a beautiful *Sacrifice of Abraham* (now in Dresden) and executed a smaller but equally perfect replica for Paolo da Terrarossa. The subsequent vicissitudes of the two pictures become very complicated in Vasari's account, but evidently the version in the Prado is the second one, given its size (a sketch for it is in the Cleveland Museum).

It is undoubtedly a late work, with a certain strength and an ordered quality. Vasari mentions with admiration "the very handsome and tender child Isaac, all nude, trembling with fear of death," the boy's robes fallen to the ground that are "real and natural" and finally the unusual landscape. If the work is read according to such naturalistic standards, the painting is certainly notable. To our sensibilities, however, the bombast in Abraham's gesture is inescapable, even accepting the intention of creating space. Nor is the excessive balance of the somewhat academic design entirely acceptable, even if we recognize a more agitated handling — a Pontormo-like sensibil-

22

RAPHAEL
Portrait of a Cardinal (1509–1510)
Panel; 2'7" × 2'.

ANDREA DEL SARTO
Florence 1486 — Florence 1531
The Sacrifice of Abraham (1525–1530)
Canvas; 3'2 1/2" × 2'3 1/4". Acquired for
Charles IV's collection at the Escorial, later
transferred to the Palace of Aranjuez.

ity — in Isaac's face and in some details of the background. There is an interesting hypothesis (R. Monti) that this work was to serve as a pendant to the *Charity* (Louvre) executed a decade earlier. It is evident that with the relaxation of the stylistic tension that reaches its maximum in a work like the *Pietà* in Vienna, Andrea del Sarto returned in the last years of his brief and intense career to his youthful tendency toward an archaizing simplicity and a more fervid religious inspiration.

ANDREA DEL SARTO. *Lucrezia del Fede.*
Traditionally it has been considered a portrait of Lucrezia whom Andrea del Fede married in 1517. It is attributable to a period a little earlier than

24

ANDREA DEL SARTO
Lucrezia del Fede (1515–1516)
Canvas; 28 3/4" × 22". The provenance is
not known. Its presence in the Spanish royal
collection is noted only since the end of the
18th century.

CORREGGIO
(ANTONIO ALLEGRI)
Correggio ca. 1489 — Correggio 1534
"Noli Me Tangere" (1522–1523)
Panel; 4'3 1/4" × 3'4 1/2". Vasari mentions
it as being in the house of the Ercolani fam-
ily in Bologna. In the 17th century it was ac-
quired by Philip IV from the collection of
Cardinal Ludovisi.

this date, because of its still Raphaelesque inspiration and because of the
mellowness of technique that may be explained by a study of Leonardo's
work. Andrea is not yet troubled by the problems posed by Michelangelo,
which subsequently impelled him along the rocky course of a break with
tradition and the recovery of individual values. The smiling portrait of Lucrezia is sister to St. Anna's elegant visitors in the famous fresco that Andrea
executed in 1514 in the Church of the Annunziata in Florence: *The Birth
of the Virgin.*

CORREGGIO. *"Noli Me Tangere."*

The work belongs to Correggio's maturity, which he reached when he was
a little over 30. A probable Roman sojourn between 1517 and 1520, or fa-
miliarity with some examples of paintings by Leonardo and Raphael, helped
him emerge from his provincial Emilian training, though that was already

illuminated by the august precedent of Mantegna's activity and was rich in originality. The painting's place lies between the refinements of the Camera della Badessa in S. Paolo and the new creative impetus of the frescoes in S. Giovanni Evangelista. A desire to break certain rigid formal schemes is felt in the twisting figures. The "variety of curves," admired even by Mengs during his Spanish sojourn, provides the images with a rhythm of undulations, echoed by the rustling wooded landscape touched by the light of dawn. The pathos typical of Correggio is seen in the intense exchange of glances between the victorious Christ and the Magdalen, who kneels, overcome by emotion.

LORENZO LOTTO
Venice ca. 1480 — Loreto 1556
Portrait of Marsilio and His Wife (1523)
Panel; 2'4" × 2'9". Signed: *"L. Lotus pictor 1523."* It appears in the inventory of 1666 as belonging to the collection of Philip IV and as hanging in his bedroom.

LORENZO LOTTO. *Portrait of Marsilio and His Wife.*
The portrait of the young married couple, dated 1523, belongs to the final phase of the Bergamesque period of Lorenzo Lotto, in which the artist found the opportunity to express himself with great freedom, breaking out

LORENZO LOTTO
St. Jerome
Panel; 3'3" × 3'11 1/2". It comes from the Monastery of the Escorial.

of classicist schemes and letting himself go in a poetic climate of fantasy influenced by Northern painting. In this period he invented an acute psychological portraiture, subtle in its humor and choice of formal means. Indeed there is an admirable coherency in the careful description of the clothes, the jewels, the nuances of expression and the gestures. The dark notes of the groom's black clothes and the sonorous chords of the red silk that adorns the bride stand out against a basic grey tone. The mischievous little cupid places a yoke decorated with laurel on their shoulders. Strange coincidence: we find the same cupid crowning a skull in the *Allegory* in the Duke of Northumberland's collection.

LORENZO LOTTO. *St. Jerome.*

On July 29, 1546, Lorenzo Lotto, recently returned to Venice after a stay in Treviso, noted in his account book that a *St. Jerome* had been delivered to Vincenzo Frigerio. This painting could be a version of the theme he noted, which was dear to him throughout his career. It may seem strange that the work could have been attributed in the past to Titian, as so many stylistic and semantic elements indicate Lotto's authorship. Yet the fact is

TITIAN
Pieve di Cadore 1488–90 — Venice 1576
St. Margaret and the Dragon (ca. 1565)
Canvas; 7'11" × 5'11 3/4". Signed: TICIANUS.
It perhaps comes from the collection of
Charles I of England. Not to be confused
with the *St. Margaret* sent by Titian to
Prince Philip in 1552, which is in the Es-
corial.

justified by Lotto's approach to Titian's creative spirit at this moment; he
was especially influenced in his portraiture. But the pathos typical of Lotto
is evident in the anxious attitude of St. Jerome adoring the crucifix. Following his custom, which is one of the many aspects that relate Lotto to the
sensibilities of Northern painting, the artist dwells on the description of a
scourge, a book and a lizard on the ground next to the saint. These details
would be enough to distance him from the spirit of Titian. Nevertheless, the
open color, saturated with light, remains Titianesque, as in another work by
Lotto, which is almost contemporary — the *Christ in Glory, with Symbols
of the Passion* in the Kunsthistorisches Museum of Vienna.

TITIAN.   *St. Margaret and the Dragon.*
Comparison with the canvas of the same subject in the Escorial, which is
documented as dating in 1552, helps us to conclude that this version was
done more than a decade later. Titian keeps the Mannerist torsion of the   **29**

saint who, with a gesture of horror — but clutching the cross — attempts to free herself from the coils of the monster.

The erect figure of the saint, illuminated by a mysterious source of light which kindles the play of complementary greens and violets of the drapery, is contrasted with the indistinct mass of monstrous coils. Only a kind of painting in which everything is built up by means of color and very free brushwork could arouse in the dark lake and the shore where menacing flames are lit an echo in nature of the cruel martyrdom.

30

TITIAN
Bacchanal (The Andrians) (1519–1520)
Canvas; 5'9" × 6'4". Signed: TICIANUS F. The second of three paintings of mythological subjects commissioned by Alfonso I d'Este to decorate his studio. In 1598 it was taken to Rome by the Cardinal Legate Aldobrandini, with the *Worship of Venus* and kept in the Palazzo Ludovisi. Monterey, Spanish Viceroy in Naples, acquired it and the *Worship of Venus* for Philip IV, and they reached the royal collection in 1639. *Bacchus and Ariadne* went to England in 1806.

TITIAN. *Bacchanal (The Andrians).*

In surviving correspondence between Titian and Alfonso d'Este can be found the dates of this masterpiece as well as the part played by the patron, who suggested for the iconography a literary text, the *Imagines* of Philostratus, which was fashionable at the court, and which Isabella d'Este had had translated. The picture describes a feast of the inhabitants of Andros, who by the grace of Dionysus, seen arriving on the ship with the white sails, are drinking at a stream of wine and praising its sweetness and strength. The figure of the sleeping nude is an intrusion of an episode of the sleeping Ariadne, abandoned by Theseus at Naxos, whom Dionysus will take with him (the subject of the *Bacchanal* in London). With the *Worship of Venus,* the three paintings form a triptych in which the pagan myth is interpreted with felicity and at the same time with extraordinary control. The study of iconographic details in the text or of formal derivations (from antique statuary for the Ariadne and from Michelangelo's cartoon of the *Battle of Cascina* for the crouching male figure) cannot overwhelm the magnificent composition of figures linked by persuasive rhythms (closed groupings alternating with dynamic lines) and by brilliant color harmonies. Going beyond the phase of classicism that was called Apollonian, Titian set out to recover its Dionysiac power.

TITIAN. *Allocution of Alfonso d'Avalos.*   *p. 32*

Pietro Aretino, in a letter of 1540, announced to d'Avalos the arrival of a little sketch of the *Allocution,* the completed version of which would be delivered to the Marquis in 1541 in Milan, where he ruled as Governor of the Duchy. It is not known whether the *Allocution* refers to a particular feat of arms. D'Avalos had distinguished himself in the struggle against the Turks, both in the Mediterranean and on the Continent. The work is interesting. The Marquis, standing with his son Ferrante, who serves him as page, addresses his troops. He wears a dark cuirass, which we know that the painter bought in Brescia as an exact model. Against the over-all darks, the reddish tones of the clothes and sky stand out. This sobriety gives greater prominence to the force of the figures, which have the authentic Mannerist stamp. The lighting has been applied to emphasize a somewhat theatrical effect. The passage suggesting the presence of the army by means of dark lances against a flashing sky has been considered a precedent for Velázquez's *Surrender of Breda.*

TITIAN. *Portrait of a Knight of Malta.*   *p. 33*

The elegant personage portrayed here by Titian has not been identified. Even his traditional designation as a "Knight of Malta" is not precise, as the cross does not correspond to the emblem of that Order. The presence of the clock suggested an identification of Giannello della Torre, clockmaker to Charles V, but this has been shown to be unfounded.

The clock, which the subject holds in his hands, has been given the symbolic value of an admonition. This would make it a unique case in Titian's portraiture, perhaps a tribute to the spirituality of Lotto. But however it may be interpreted as allusion, the model appears to be unaffected; he has an exuberant physical vitality, emphasized by a sumptuousness of dress that indicates high social rank. The full healthy face has a composed expression;

TITIAN
Allocution of Alfonso d'Avalos (1540–1541)
Canvas; 7'3" × 5'5". It belonged to the collection of Charles I of England, perhaps having come from Mantua; in Spain at least since 1666.

the lively eyes smile. The figure has been masterfully placed in space, in an atmosphere created solely by means of color and airy brushwork permeated with light. The work certainly cannot be dated earlier than 1550.

And as for the clock-symbol, we should not forget that it also appears in the *Portrait of Salvaresio* of 1558. Thus it perhaps was a valuable gift made to the painter and kept as an ornament in his studio, which was frequented by princes and kings.

TITIAN. *Charles V on Horseback.* *p. 34*
Titian's portraiture was particularly intense in the second half of the decade 1540–50. During his Roman sojourn in '45, the Pope had sat for him several times. An unforgettable page in his career is the *Paul III and His Neph-*

TITIAN
Portrait of a Knight of Malta
Canvas; 4' × 3'3 3/4". Provenance: Royal Palace of Madrid. It belonged to the collection of Charles II, and was saved from the fire of 1734.

TITIAN
Venus and the Organ Player (ca. 1550)
Canvas; 4′5 1/2″ × 7′2 1/2″. Inventoried for
the first time in the catalogue of the Alcazar
in Madrid, in 1666. It may have come from
the collection of Charles I of England, as a
similar composition appears in van Dyck's
sketch book. In the Prado since 1827.

ews, a psychological study of three personalities, of a world, of an epoch.
It is not surprising that the Emperor called Titian to Augsburg — where
he had convoked the Diet and was staying with his splendid court and the
feudatories of his vast empire — to serve as official portraitist. To handle
the numerous commissions, Titian had brought with him his son Orazio,
Cesare Vecellio and an able follower, Lamberto Sustris. The portrait of
Charles V, however, was executed by Titian himself, and in a quite short
time — from April to September 1548. It is a portrait commemorating the
Battle of Mülberg of 1547, in which the Emperor had defeated the Protestant princes. The image of the Emperor, however, is not that of a victorious
hero. It is the symbol of a strength of will that commits the individual to
contend against enormous forces, that goads him on, consumes him. We do
not know how much awareness there was in the artist in creating this his-
toric interpretation, but there is no ambiguity in the reading of the picture,
and his splendid series of portraits of famous people assures us that Titian
possessed the ability to penetrate men and human events. The colors are
darkling, perhaps emphasized by restorations that followed the damage in-
curred in a fire in the 18th century. The brushwork that builds up the sumptuous armor, the severe face, is laid on heavily. The heraldic disposition of
the knight on horseback is exemplary.

TITIAN. *Venus and the Organ Player.*
The reclining nude leans on one elbow and amuses herself with a little dog.
The elegant gentleman interrupts his concert to turn and look, one hand on

TITIAN
Charles V on Horseback (1548)
Canvas; 10′10 1/2″ × 9′2″.

35

the keyboard. There is apparent here a desire to stop a moment containing both the past and the future. The account is continued beyond the marble balustrade, in the landscape with its avenue of trees, fountain, the stags and does wandering free; a couple goes off into the background distance, animated by the light of a setting sun. The splendor of the scene, the elegance of the man, the beauty of the nude — calm and sure — the hint of music still sounding in the room — are almost emblematic elements of a concept of life as art. It might border on banality if it were not achieved in terms of high formal invention, from composition to color; if it were not felt that the sensuality finds completion in an intuition of nature. The flashing highlights on the dark tones of the velvet bed cover and the curtain remind us of solutions adopted by Tintoretto. The woman's face also departs from Titian's classic modules. Some studio assistants' work can be recognized in unimportant details.

TITIAN. *Danaë*.

From letters between Titian and the court of Madrid, it has been established that this *Danaë* was executed in 1553. The painting takes up again a subject done in 1546 (now in Naples). The figure of the young woman is posed reclining on a bed, and her beautiful body, recalling elegant Mannerist proportions, turns with a lazy rhythm towards us; her glance is directed

36

Right: detail.
TITIAN
Danaë (1553)
Canvas; 4′2 3/4″ × 5′10 3/4″. The painting is one of the "poems" Titian composed for Prince Philip, which reached Madrid at the beginning of 1554, a year before Philip succeeded to the throne of Spain.

up to the cloud, from which Jove pours a shower of gold down on his be-
loved mortal. In place of the classic cupid, we find here the disagreeable
figure of an old servant who avidly holds out her apron to catch some of
the coins — a sad figure that appears in many of the seduction scenes of
the time. A comparison with the earlier version, which was painted in
Rome, gives us some light on the development of Titian's taste. In 1546 he
appears to be engaged in an effort that is classic in tone and the composition works to suggest space. In this version it is the color imbued with light
which resolves the problem of form. The light, descending fantastically from
the cloud, is not only a part of the plot, but a great stylistic solution.

TITIAN
Venus and Adonis (1553)
Canvas; 6'1 1/4" × 6'9 1/2". It was sent to London in 1554 for Prince Philip, on the occasion of his marriage to Mary Tudor, but was intended for the dressing room in the palace in Madrid, where the *Danaë* had already been hung.

TITIAN.   *Venus and Adonis.*

The work is mentioned in a letter from Titian to Prince Philip and was enthusiastically praised by Ludovico Dolce in his dialogue on painting (1557). Titian's creation is not only a complex of images that are beautiful in themselves and full of vitality, as Dolce, with his fully naturalistic Renaissance taste, understood, but it is a dramatic concept achieved with great stylistic coherence. The possession of a rich and subtle command of color, the ability to bend the substance of the color to the most intense tonalities and the most refined nuances, permit Titian to place his figures in open space and articulate their contrapuntal movements — the impatient movement of the young hunter, the tender gesture of Venus, who attempts to hold him back, are almost a presage of the imminent tragedy. And meanwhile there are the dogs, "so naturally painted they seem to sniff, bay and be full of eagerness to confront any wild beast" (L. Dolce). Titian explained to Philip II that he had represented Venus from the back to distinguish her from the Danaë, which was to be its companion piece. Very likely, however, the painter has taken up a Hellenistic Maenad motive, echoed for example in the famous bas-relief of the *Ara Grimani,* which could be admired in the Venetian palace of the same name in the S. Maria Formosa district.

TITIAN.   *The Entombment.*   *pp. 40–41*

The canvas was commissioned by Philip II in 1559 and was sent to him in the same year. It has capital importance in the development of Titian's style. The portrayal of the tragedy, which the painter had masterfully achieved in epic form in a youthful work now in the Louvre, is here shown in terms of a living, suffering participation to which the pictorial language is extraordinarily appropriate. It is significant that the bearded Joseph of Arimathea, who supports the body of Christ, is more than probably a self-portrait. Knowingly composed, the figures are distributed in a fan-like scheme and are racked by spasms of grief. But it is the color that controls all the elements, starting from the livid body of Christ and from the white shroud falling over the side of the tomb, which is decorated with bas-reliefs. The last are the only unessential, ornamental notes in this tragic group. The bloodless body of Christ and the weight of His listless arm are unforgettable. Unforgettable, too, is the figure of the Magdalen. Most extraordinary, however, is how color creates the individual figures, so that the space is reduced, attenuated and leaves us breathless. Dvoràk rightly suggested that in this moment Titian, "renouncing the intoxication of the senses of his youthful works, had sought to find himself in a higher and more remote region of the spirit."

There is much to say about Titian's sense of religion, which is not to be confused with any didactic or pietistic zeal of the type that activated Counter-Reformation policy in the arts and was urged on him by some patrons — as exemplified in a canvas in the Prado titled *Spain Succoring Religion* which in fact consists of two feminine beauties counterpoised, one richly dressed, the other nude. Yet a dramatic concept of humanity in terms of its myths and its history, and of the nature that seems to echo it, is more and more apparent in the works of the last period, from the late *Entombment* and *St. Lawrence,* also in the Prado, to the *St. Sebastian* in Leningrad and *Apollo and Marsyas* in Kormeríz, Czechoslovakia.

Pages 40–41:
TITIAN
The Entombment (1559)
Canvas; 4'6" × 5'9". Signed: *"Titianus Vecellius aeques."*

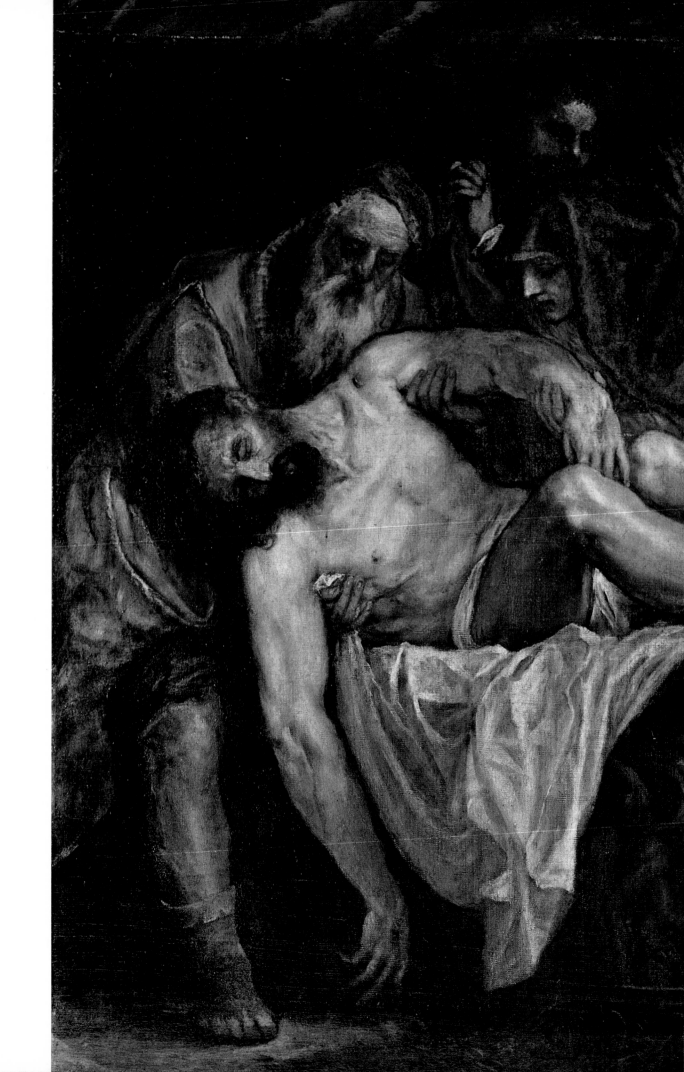

TITIAN. *Adam and Eve.*

It is difficult to judge Titian's image of the *Original Sin*. Strange that this theme, which should have been congenial, is represented only by this single example in the artist's production. Nothing is known of the history of the picture, which has been in the chapel of the Alcazar, Madrid, for no one knows how long. It was damaged by fire in 1734 and subsequently underwent a heavy-handed restoration by the painter Juan de Miranda.

Critics for the most part agree that it was executed around 1560–70, but following an iconographic theme of the artist's youth, or even worked on a canvas laid out many years earlier. In fact the bodies are defined in a grandiose way. The figure of Eve especially is strikingly monumental and dominates the space with its luminous mass. There is a narrative suggestion in Adam's gesture, with which he tries to prevent his companion from accepting the forbidden fruit from Lilith. Adam's limbs, disposed with a calm rhythm, have a fullness whose weight is not diminished by the enveloping atmosphere. The sturdy tree trunk and lush foliage balance the massive figures of the protagonists. The most melting, atmospheric passage is in the fantastic mountain landscape, seen as if from some inaccessible summit — the mythical Eden where the temptation takes place.

TITIAN
Adam and Eve (ca. 1560–1565)
Canvas; 7'10 1/2" × 6'1 1/4". Signed *"Titianus F."* It comes from the chapel of the Alcazar in Madrid, was in the collection of Philip II and figures in the inventory of 1663, when it was in the palace chapel.

JACOPO TINTORETTO. *Battle of Corsairs.* pp. 44–45

This subject has been variously interpreted; the painting itself was brought to Madrid by Velázquez, who had been ordered by King Philip IV to collect the most beautiful works to be found in Italy (1649–51). A suggested identification with a *Battle* painted by Tintoretto for Ercole Gonzaga in 1562 is belied by the stylistic evidence; this is a much later work. Behind it is a long experience in the composition of masses in motion and the distribution of light effects, such as those adopted by Tintoretto in the great canvases in the ground-floor of the Scuola di S. Rocco. Similar problems, sharing the same iconographic points of departure, are resolved by the painter in the series of the *Annals of the Gonzaga* and in many commemorative canvases in the Palazzo Ducale, Venice.

All evidence dates the work around 1580. However, while in the series of the *Annals* and in the Palazzo Ducale Tintoretto employed considerable studio assistance, this battle of corsairs gives the impression that the hand of Jacopo predominated. The control — still Renaissance in character — that we find even in Tintoretto's most uninhibited compositional fantasies can be noted in the contained quality of the gestures, which is very far from the rhetoric that will be typical of the Baroque. The quality of the technique is high, as seen in the transparency of the flesh of the woman captive in the foreground. Profoundly skillful is the relationship between foreground and background, where figures are reduced to incandescent filaments. Admirable above all is the strict register of the light effects.

Pages 44–45:

JACOPO TINTORETTO
Battle of Corsairs (Abduction of Helen) (ca. 1580)
Canvas; 6' × 10'. Listed under the second title in the 1666 inventory of the Royal Palace of Madrid.

JACOPO TINTORETTO
Venice 1518 — Venice 1594
The Finding of Moses (ca. 1550–1555)
Canvas; 1'10" × 3'11". Bought in Venice by
Velázquez for King Philip IV.

JACOPO TINTORETTO
Joseph and Potiphar's Wife (ca. 1550–1555)
Canvas; 1'9 1/4" × 3'10". Bought in Venice
by Velázquez for Philip IV.

It is perhaps useful to recall that the taste for epic descriptions, for battles, which in the succeeding century became a true and proper genre, had its enthusiastic pioneers: it was in 1581 that Tasso published his celebrated poem, *Gerusalemme Liberata.*

JACOPO TINTORETTO. *The Finding of Moses.*
With six other biblical scenes — *Judith and Holofernes, Susanna and the Elders, The Queen of Sheba before Solomon, Esther before Ahasuerus, Joseph and Potiphar's Wife, The Purification of the Midianite Virgins* (unfortunately damaged and repainted) — it made up the decoration of a ceiling in a palace in Venice, where Velázquez bought them, during his second Venetian sojourn, for Philip IV. The centerpiece must have been the *Purification of the Midianite Virgins,* as the Spanish historian, Palomino de Castro, clearly states; the other rectangular canvases formed a frieze around it. The decorative sumptuousness of the paintings, the illusionistic perspective frameworks and the rich color call for a fairly early dating: the years between 1550 and 1555, when Tintoretto came closest to Paolo Veronese. This work in particular, with its harmonious rhythm of the figures linked by broad curvilinear cadences echoed by the branches bending over the group in which Moses is at dead center, reminds us of Veronese's modules. Though these stem from Mannerism, they are quieted by the instinct for equilibrium typical of Paolo, in whom Tintoretto found inspiration at this moment.

We are far from the violence of the first perspective experiments inspired by Mantuan examples, which Tintoretto had carried out in the notable series of ceiling paintings for a Venetian palace — a series that is now in the Galleria Estense, Modena.

JACOPO TINTORETTO. *Joseph and Potiphar's Wife.*
This painting is one of the smaller parts of the frieze that decorated the ceiling of a Venetian palace, from which it was bought with the other six canvases in the same series by Velázquez, who had been sent by Philip IV to Italy to acquire pictures for the Royal Collection. The Spanish master must have been particularly pleased by the richness and luminosity of the work and the immediacy with which the brush translates the mental image of the artist on to the canvas.

The composition is felicitous — asymmetrical, mobile and constructed around two divergent lines created by the velvet curtain and the figure of Joseph, who pulls violently away from the beautiful reclining nude. The perspective construction, by which the composition is seen from a very low viewpoint, creates a slight feeling of vertigo. It is this idea of space that typifies Tintoretto's creative character. If it is Mannerism, in particular through his relationship to Giulio Romano in Mantua, that gives the Venetian painter the means for these flights of imagination, we also must recognize that Tintoretto makes use of it admirably. He rendered his own spiritual anxiety as well as that of his time. To return to an analysis of the color, whose quality is so high in this moment of contact with Veronese, one is struck by the nude Potiphar's wife, defined by a sinuous but tense line, which emanates an extraordinary luminosity counterpointed by the dark green of the alcove and the silken materials that are traversed by shining flickers.

PAOLO VERONESE. *Venus and Adonis.*

Certainly a genius in painting, Paolo Veronese maintained from the beginning to the end of his career a number of constant factors. As interpreter of certain aspirations of the culture of his time, he risked alienation from the deepest and most uneasy currents of 16th century spirituality, pursuing his own ideal of formal perfection, which in the end is an escape. The last of Paolo's production (1570–88), however, is touched by a breath of pathos and reflects the need for meditation, which is evident not only in his choice of themes but in the evolution of his style. But noble images were also produced in this period, such as the allegorical fables painted for Rudolph II and this idyll of Venus and Adonis. "The two protagonists are lost in the same enchantment as Tasso's Rinaldo and Amida," as R. Pallucchini says. And this is true especially for the enchanted atmosphere in which the artist immersed his figures: the diaphanously luminous Venus, Adonis relaxed in sleep, Cupid holding back the impatient dog. There is not, however, as in Tasso's poetry, a dramatic motive to Paolo Veronese's escapism. To appreciate this it is enough to compare the thematic development of Titian's *Venus and Adonis,* with its presentiment of death, and the somewhat fatuous gesture of Venus waving her fan and watching over her sleeping lover in Paolo's version. Certainly his classical inclinations, after the dissipation of his energies as a colorist in such canvases as the *Marriage of St. Catherine* and the *Rape of Europa* in the Palazzo Ducale, here again recover their beautiful equilibrium.

PAOLO VERONESE. *The Finding of Moses.* *p. 50*

This small painting is the twin of one in the National Gallery of Washington, even to the dimensions. It must have been much admired, as there are other replicas — although none on this high level — which are in the museums of Dresden and Dijon. It is certainly later than the Prado's *Venus and Adonis.* The dimensions themselves permit the painter an intensity of exceptional color effects, without however reaching the feeling of satiety noticeable in some of the preceding courtly compositions.

The charm of Paolo Veronese's rare small-sized compositions, which were created for refined patrons, could be compared to a musician, accustomed to the symphonic power of the organ, improvising delicate variations on a spinet. To continue the musical metaphor, the composition flows along in continuously legato rhythms, from the figure of the slave to the young girl handing the child to Pharaoh's daughter and her elderly companion, while three other figures at the right repeat the stepped succession of the group. The counterpoint in color is varied and rich. A diverting note is the portrayal of the Egyptian city, with temples, towers and pinnacles — a fantasy spun from the complicated sensibilities of Mannerism.

GIOVAN BATTISTA MORONI. *Portrait.* *p. 51*

Although the activity of Moroni, disciple of Moretto da Brescia, includes religious scenes, the painter's fame is connected with the series of portraits he executed during his Brescian period, which lasted until 1553, as well as after his return to Bergamo, where he acquired a vast clientele. Titian himself recommended Moroni for his "naturalness" to a gentleman of the Al-

PAOLO VERONESE
Verona 1528 — Venice 1588
Venus and Adonis (ca. 1570–1575)
Canvas; 6'11 1/2" ×6'4 1/4". Acquired by Velázquez in Venice for Philip IV.

GIOVAN BATTISTA MORONI
Albino (Bergamo) 1523? — Albino 1578
Portrait (ca. 1560)
Canvas; 3'10 3/4" × 2'11 3/4". In 1666 it
figures in a list of paintings in the Alcazar,
Madrid.

bani family. In fact it is inescapable that he has a particular ability to approach reality directly, which goes back to a Lombard tradition and relates him to other great contemporary artists of similar experience but belonging to the Venetian world: Lotto, Savoldo and Romanino. Some compositions in the Mannerist taste appear to have been filtered through Venetian styles, as in the *Portrait of a Poet*, 1560, in the Pinacoteca Tosio Martinengo, Brescia. Our portrait is considered to be of the same period. In Moroni's gallery of personalities, who are for the most part unknown, but who reveal their social positions and specific trades or professions — the tailor, the lawyer — this one is considered "the official." A consciousness of authority emanates from the personage, from his golden collar that stands out on the rich garb, from the severity of the entire composition, both from the point of view of color and from the sober architectural reference.

PAOLO VERONESE
The Finding of Moses (1570–1575)
Canvas; 19 3/4" × 17". From the collection
of Philip IV.

51

GIAMBATTISTA TIEPOLO. *The Immaculate Conception.*

On March 31, 1762, Tiepolo left for Madrid with his sons Domenico and Lorenzo, on the invitation of Charles III, to fresco the throne room. This demanding commission was successfully carried out and the Venetian was asked to decorate other halls. Then there seems to have been a halt in Tiepolo's production in 1765–66, and in 1767 the painter asked the court for more work. Despite the obvious hostility of the King's Confessor, Padre de Electa, and the manifest rivalry of other painters — among them Mengs — he obtained an order to execute seven large canvases for the church of S. Pascual de Aranjuez. *The Immaculate Conception* belongs to this series, which is religious not only in iconographic theme but also in interior motivation. The subject was not new to Tiepolo. He took up again the iconography of the altarpiece now in the museum of Vicenza: a representation of the Virgin as a celestial being crushing underfoot a serpent that is attacking the earth, while angels adore her. A stylistic comparison throws light on the evolution of Tiepolo's style in the last years of his career. In the Vicenza altarpiece, datable around 1735, the Virgin is solidly constructed, following a module of Piazzetta's. Her white garment seems to emit flashes, and the violence of the light and shade also throws the soft limbs of the cupids into strong relief. In the Madrid picture, all violence is gone. Light emanates without combustion and discreet little angels lean adoringly from the soft cloud. The ascending motion of the Virgin is accentuated, and around her the mantle swells and palpitates, like a sail filling with wind. A very fine sketch for the painting is in London, in the collection of Lord Kinnaird.

GIAMBATTISTA TIEPOLO
Venice 1696 — Madrid 1770
The Immaculate Conception (ca. 1767–1769)
Canvas; 9'2" × 4'11 3/4". Signed: *"Dn. Juan Batta Tiepolo inv. et pinx."* Painted for the church of San Pascual of Aranjuez. In the Prado since 1828.

GIAMBATTISTA TIEPOLO. *The Triumph of Venus.*   *p. 54*

We do not know whether this splendid sketch served for the execution of a ceiling for the "Court of Muscovy" on which Tiepolo worked in the autumn of 1761, a year before his departure for Spain. Stylistically it is close to the sketches for the Madrid ceilings, which are now in the museums of Cambridge and Boston. If our sensibility occasionally finds it difficult to enjoy the spectacular ability of Tiepolo in his grand fresco compositions, and if this awkward feeling is complicated by thoughts on the character of the painter, who was devoted to the exaltation of unstable powers and discredited myths, our reservations fall away before the felicity of his sketches. The ability of the Venetian tradition to achieve with color and light a semblance of reality and absolute creations of the imagination found its last incarnations in the magisterial quality of Tiepolo's forms and in the lyricism of Guardi's *vedute*. Venus goes by lounging in a carriage drawn by doves and escorted by cupids. Mercury, sketched in a few rapid strokes, descends from on high, while Minerva and Saturn below, seen against a white wall which accentuates the perspective, observe the procession. The most enchanting passage is that of the Three Graces who, from their throne of white clouds, offer their rosy nudity to our view. Here again is the miracle of a light that does not destroy but exalts form, that does not imitate reality but transfigures it. A fine engraving of the composition was executed by Tiepolo's son Lorenzo.

Page 54:

GIAMBATTISTA TIEPOLO
The Triumph of Venus (ca. 1726–1765)
Canvas; 2'9" × 2' 1/4". Sketch for a lost ceiling; in the Prado since 1834.

SPAIN

THE MASTER OF ZAFRA. *St. Michael the Archangel.*

The signature on the sword is believed to be that of the armorer. The work has been attributed to the painter Juan Sanchez de Castro or a follower of his, but with little basis. There are Flemish elements in the band of angels and in the diabolical figures below, which recall Bosch, but do not have his crystalline details. A Flemish manner is also evident in the large figure of the Archangel, but the regular forms of the armor and head also suggest an Italian influence. The determining factor is the composition, which is clearly and rigorously architectonic even in the rich imagery that crowds the margins of the panel. The oblong form is divided by two diagonals on which is constructed the straddling figure of the Archangel; this is closed off above in an angular arrangement, around which rotates a large ellipse descending from the mantle to the wing of the infernal dragon below. Despite the dense pulsation of the little figures emerging on every side, this simple, immediate format — which allows the viewer to follow the central figure in its surging upward development — sums up the whole image. In the mirroring center of the shield is reflected the lateral scene in which a demon and a guardian angel fight for the soul of the donor of the work. The Master of Zafra is certainly one of the best artists working in Spain around 1475, and his technical performance has a rare refinement.

BARTOLOMÉ DE CARDENAS BERMEJO. *San Domingo de Silos.*

The stylistic language of Bartolomé Bermejo is clearly Flemish, from his first known work (a *St. Michael* now in the Ludlow collection), to the *Pietà* in the Cathedral of Barcelona, dated 1490. The place and nature of his training, and perhaps also his early activity, are to be sought among the artists of Tournai and of Rogier, and immediately afterwards in the vicinity of Dirk Bouts (1420–75). Bouts's influence is seen in this magnificent *San Domingo* enthroned within a Gothic construction decorated with fabulous towers, pinnacles and niches containing the seven cardinal Virtues — Strength, Justice, Charity, Prudence, Temperance, Faith and Hope, in the form of women sumptuously dressed in multicolored robes. The figure of St. Dominick, the great promoter of the Faith, with his book and elaborately worked pastoral, is presented in a strict frontal position and is constructed from triangles, in accordance with the canons of Gothic architecture. The cope embroidered with figures, with its thickness and weight, accentuates the impression of a large statue placed on the imposing carved throne; and above, the jeweled mitre starts the upward surge of the spires. In other works the dominating preference is for intensely dramatic and agitated subjects, like the *Descent into Limbo* (in the museum in Barcelona), which recalls Bouts's infernos, with their shrieking nudes and monsters. In this panel everything is apparently motionless — to create the majesty of an icon — but the various elements and details, worked up with almost unflagging exasperation, show the character of the master's imagination. With Nuño Gonçalvez he was among the greatest Iberian artists of his time.

56

THE MASTER OF ZAFRA
St. Michael the Archangel (ca. 1475)
Tempera on panel; 7'11 1/4" × 5'1/4".
Provenance: Hospital of San Miguel, Zafra
(Andalusia); acquired by the Prado in 1924.

BARTOLOMÉ BERMEJO
(RUBEUS)
Born in Cordova, active from
1474 to 1498(?)
San Domingo de Silos (1477)
Tempera on panel; 7'11 1/4" × 4'3 1/4". The
central part of an altarpiece for which the
artist was commissioned on September 5,
1474; the panel was completed by November
17, 1477. In 1869–1871, in the Archeologi-
cal Museum, Madrid; since 1920 in the
Prado.

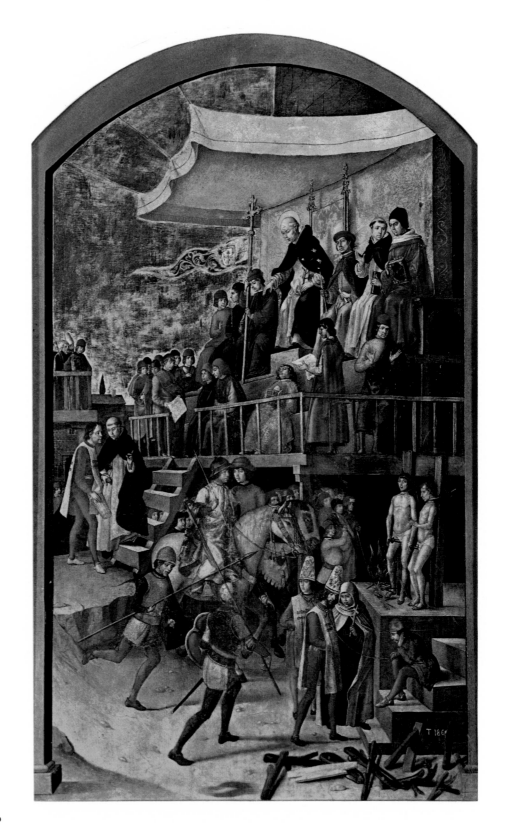

PEDRO BERRUGUETE
Paredes de Nava (?) (Palencia); in Urbino
in 1477; died before January 5, 1504.
St. Dominick Presiding over an Auto da Fé
Tempera on panel; 5′1/2″ × 3′1/4″. From
the sacristy of Santo Tomás of Avila, where
there was a companion panel. Acquired for
the museum in 1867; a similar panel is
known to have been in a private collection
in London.

PEDRO BERRUGUETE.   *St. Dominick Presiding over an Auto da Fé.*
After an initial Hispano-Flemish training, Pedro Berruguete established his
style in Urbino, where he worked extensively for Duke Frederico II, Piero   59

della Francesco's great patron. His activity at Avila came after his sojourn in Italy. The influence from Urbino (including Francesco di Giorgio's) is clear in the perspective plan and in the arrangement of diagonals and stepped planes. The principal masses are — below — the circle around the condemned (with the fine detail of the scattered logs in the foreground) and — above — the bulk of the tribune where the judges are seated under a canopy. Within the structure, which is divided in two directions, upwards and downwards, from the left, with the floor beam of the tribune serving as linchpin, Berruguete has placed animated figures, whose elegant, dramatic gestures neutralize the ferocious character of the subject.

60

LUIS MORALES
("EL DIVINO")
Badajoz ca. 1500 — Badajoz 1586
Madonna and Child
Oil on panel; 2'9" × 2'1 1/4".
P. Bosch Bequest.

FERNANDO YAÑES
DE LA ALMEDINA
Almedina (Ciudad Real); in Italy before 1505; active at Valencia in 1505–1506 and at Cuenca from 1526 to 1531–1536.
St. Catherine
Oil on panel; 6'11 1/2" × 3'8". Acquired from the Argudin family in 1946.

FERNANDO YAÑEZ DE LA ALMEDINA. *St. Catherine.*
Recognized as the work of Yañez by Tormo in 1915, it is considered the most beautiful Spanish canvas of the 16th century. With Fernando de los Llanos, Vicente Mancip (educated in Venice under Bonifazio and Bordone), Juan de Juanes, Pedro Machuca and Alonso Berruguete (a follower of Rosso), the artist is held to be one of the major representatives of Spanish Italianism. This work may be dated in the early years of the 16th century, after the artist's return from Italy, where he studied Leonardo's chiaroscuro effects for markedly sculptural shapes, occasionally resorting to antiquity for inspiration. The painter rarely departed from models accepted as "classical." But his art has its penetrating moments, in the rendering of physical movement and especially in the often "highly charged" heads.

LUIS DE MORALES. *Madonna and Child.*
An image typical of the painter, who was famous among his contemporaries for his attention to the psychological traits of saints and other sacred personages. With an indirectly Italian training, via Dutch Mannerism, Morales preferred representations with a marked emotional accent, and he accentuated their pathetic or effusive character. In this work, the subject — derived from Raphael and Correggio — of the agitated body and the encircling arms forming a cylindrical block is emphasized by the Madonna's head, Raphaelesque both as module and in its delicate, restrained beauty. More original are the icy, metallic colors that grade into the shadows.

EL GRECO. *The Annunciation.* *p. 62*
This splendid little panel is one of the first works of Theotokopoulos, and was certainly painted in Venice (prior to 1570) before he moved to Spain. It reflects the pictorial language of his master, Titian. Yet there is already a prophecy of his mature style in the vivid contrasts of light and shadow, in the agitated, flickering shapes assimilated to lights (as in the angels around the Holy Ghost in the upper part of the picture) and at the end of the perspective where the buildings flash against the sky. In all this, along with his understanding of the "tragic" style of the aged Titian, there is shown a leaping imagination and a power of rapture that will emerge shortly afterward in his first Toledan works.

EL GRECO. *The Holy Trinity.* *p. 63*
This is El Greco's first work executed in Toledo, 1577–79. On clouds which seem to be rising and swelling, a scene of extraordinarily intense and unexpected drama takes place. God the Father surrounded by angels raises the body of the dead Christ; the vision of His martyrdom is superimposed on that of the majestic religious symbol. In this canvas, too, the relationship to the late Titian is close, but he also uses Tintoretto (who is recalled in the soft bodies with their dancers' movements: note the angel seen from behind) in the tense contrapositions. He adapts a device originating with Dürer which Michelangelo used in his *Pietà:* the body of Christ is made

EL GRECO
(DOMENIKOS THEOTOKOPOULOS)
Born in Candia in 1541; in Venice in 1566;
in Rome 1570–1571; in Venice 1572; in
Madrid ? 1575–1576; in Toledo 1577; died
in Toledo, 1614.
The Annunciation
Oil on panel; 10 1/4″ × 7 1/2″. Acquired
for the museum in 1868; formerly in the
Academia de San Fernando.

triangular and serpentine. El Greco transfigures the Michelangelesque idea
into a torsion which is almost painfully forced at every point. This idea was
never published in prints, so we must assume that the artist reconstructed
an image that comes between the *Pietà* of the Duomo of Florence and the
one in Palestrina, which perhaps he had seen in Rome in 1570–72 (or drawings for them). With this work, Greco began the brilliant cycle of his mature work.

EL GRECO. *The Adoration of the Shepherds.*
The formal theme of this work, which is among the most moving produc-
tions of the end of Greco's career, is the bell-shaped space created in the
middle of the composition. Around it are disposed the figures — with their
seemingly automatic movements — below the Holy Family and the ador-

EL GRECO
The Holy Trinity (1577)
Oil on canvas; 9'10" × 5'10 1/2". From the altarpiece of Santo Domingo el Antiguo in Toledo, where it (and the *Assumption* in the Chicago Art Institute) formed the upper part. Executed in 1577. Acquired 1827.

EL GRECO
Adoration of the Shepherds
Oil on canvas; 10'6" × 5'10 3/4". Entered the museum in 1954.

ing shepherds. Above, on similar crossed paths, cupids and angels rotate as if blown by the wind, where the clouds break up into tufts or mass together. Meanwhile, the convergence of the pattern made by the angel and the shepherd on the right accentuates the impetus that carries every part of the composition toward the luminous Child, above the crescent-shaped horn of the ox.

Ascetic and inspired, in the elongated, flexible shapes of Greco's last period, the figures move in every direction. The brushwork and rapid strokes of color fluctuate without pause, as in a vortex, to suggest a double view from below and above, rising and sinking, that opens to a dazzling center. The work was executed for the church of San Domingo el Antiguo, Toledo, between 1603 and 1607.

EL GRECO. *Baptism of Christ.*

An accentuated, almost dizzying verticality develops in three leaps from the ground, from the kneeling Christ to the flight of angels to the symbol of the Holy Ghost. Compositional elements derived from Italian sources (linked diagonals, connection by means of triangular and rectangular figures, converging and diverging ellipses) persist, but these themes are invested with a new impetus by the pictorial technique which burns like a fuse over the surface. All traditional rules of painting are broken. The artist alters or contradicts dimensions, creates protruding masses or deep chasms on the canvas, pushes relationships almost to the breaking point. The picture is not frontal; it penetrates in a swift diagonal toward the upper part of the

EL GRECO
Baptism of Christ
Oil on canvas; 11'6" × 4'8 3/4". Detail of the lower part. Signed in Greek. Painted for the collegiate church of the Augustinians of Doña Maria de Aragon in Madrid: the contract is dated 1596; the painting was delivered in 1600.

EL GRECO
The Resurrection
Oil on canvas; 9'1/4" × 4'2". Signed at lower right, in Greek. Companion piece to the *Pentecost* (see pages 69–70–71). A canvas of this theme is mentioned as being in the church of the Virgen de Atocha, Madrid. Provenance: Museo de la Trinidad.

composition. The thrust is accompanied by leaps or jumps which — if they still have Tintoretto as an antecedent — are produced in new ways. Light traverses the image with a kaleidoscopic variety and transmutes masses of color and texture into radiance.

EL GRECO. *The Resurrection.*   *p. 65*

Although it has been dated even later than 1600, this picture more likely dates around 1584–94. Christ with His banner, surrounded by an aura of light, forms a sort of wedge that is perpendicularly aligned with the axis of the lower part of the composition. There the eight figures of the soldiers are disposed along diagonals that are centrifugal to the central axis, and in rapid, violent *contrapposto* they fall over, flee or draw back — struck by the splendor of the Resurrected. The wedging in of the bodies is equal to the impetus of their precipitous movements caught at the climactic moment, in contrast with the composed, serene figure of Christ suspended in mid-air. The atmosphere below is charged with tempestuous light; the illumination is also instantaneous, as from a flash of lightning. Here, too, Italian reminiscences, from Tintoretto to Michelangelo, give Greco clues and points of departure for a symphonic poetry that is both epic and lyric.

EL GRECO. *St. Andrew and St. Francis.*

The conversation between the two saints takes place on either side of St. Andrew's cross, which forms two spaces in which the figures are placed in correspondence, both in rhythm and composition. The figures are in mobile, unstable positions; they skim the ground almost precariously, their feet moving in dance steps, a motion repeated by their gestures. Behind them, the yawning void of the sky is dappled with lights and darks. The intimate conversation is transposed into a dialogue of visual forms.

EL GRECO. *The Crucifixion.*   *pp. 68–69*

In this work of around 1600, the elongated vertical format persists, giving the spectator's visual path a prolonged temporal quality, involving sequences, accelerations, pauses, interruptions and diversions both on the surface and in depth. Greco was a most attentive and complex inventor of spectacular compositions, which have nothing of the schematic or repetitious. They continually renew their powers of suggestion through the strenuous search for new forms of representation, within a cultural framework (to which should be added here, as elsewhere, the experience of Parmigianino). He never negated his Italian experience, even when he turned it around or transposed it in highly personal, compellingly original results. In this work, which is faithful to a familiar iconographic tradition, it is enough to observe the descent of the forms on the right, picked up and reinforced by the extraordinarily suspended angel seen from the back, in order to understand the artist's power of imagination.

EL GRECO. *The Pentecost.*   *pp. 69–70–71*

Although believed by some scholars to belong to the group which includes *The Baptism, The Pentecost* documents a later stylistic moment, between 1604 and 1614. In a still violently elongated format, the vision opens

Left: Detail.
EL GRECO
St. Andrew and St. Francis
Oil on canvas; 5'5 3/4" × 3'8 1/2". Signed on piece of paper represented at lower right. Donated to the Monasterio de la Encarnación, Madrid, in 1676; acquired by the Prado in 1942.

66

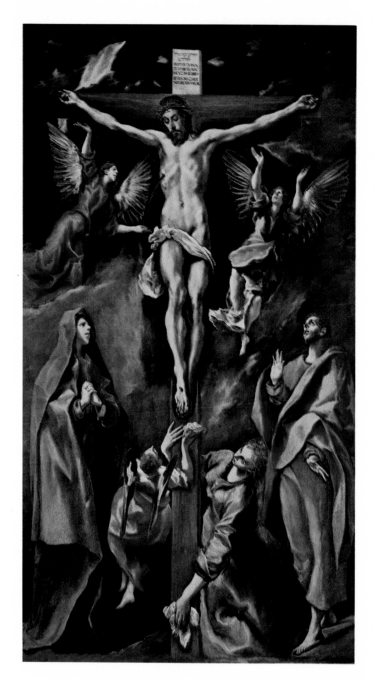

EL GRECO
The Crucifixion
Oil on canvas; 10'2 1/2" × 5'6 1/2".
Signed below the Cross, in Greek.
It probably comes from the Jesuit
church of San Juan Bautista
in Toledo (1836).

EL GRECO
Pentecost
Oil on canvas; 9'1/4" × 4'2".
Signed on the step, in Greek.
Pendant to the *Resurrection* (see page 65).
From the Museo de la Trinidad.
Pages 70–71: Detail.

steeply upward, with a kind of burning impetus reinforced by flashing colors,
from the agitated apostles to the apparently frontal group of the Madonna
among the disciples of Christ (the next to the last figure to the right seems
to be a portrait and resembles Covarrubias). There is an indescribable, impassioned agitation around the figure of the Virgin, heightened by the figures and forms compressed in a narrow space that reverberates beyond the
vortex made by the apostles struck by the miraculous event. El Greco
pushes his burning imagination to the point of fragmenting the color,
breaching the vibrant margins and applying the brushwork in a vehement
jet that maintains the flaming inspiration of the artist.

JUAN BAUTISTA MAINO
Born in the territory of Milan in 1568; in
Toledo from 1611; died in Madrid, 1649.
*The Reconquest of Bahia in Brazil; Don
Fadrique de Toledo presents the colony with
a tapestry representing Philip IV between the
Conde-Duque de Olivares and Victory; on
the ground the corpses of Heresy, Ire and
War.*

Oil on canvas; 10′1 3/4″ × 12′6 1/4″.
Painted for the Salon de Reinos del Palacio
del Buen Retiro, Madrid; commemorates the
victory of Don Fadriques de Toledo (beside
him are his lieutenant Don Juan de Orellana
and the Admiral Don Juan Fajardo de Gue-
vara) on May 1, 1626, the *ante quem* date
for the painting.

On page 73: detail.

JUAN BAUTISTA MAINO. *The Reconquest of Bahia.*
The "historical" and commemorative part of this large canvas was merely
an excuse for the work, and includes only the right side and the background
with the fleet at anchor in the bay and the soldiers and Indians on the beach.
The real center of interest is the scene in the left foreground, where 13 figures enact the succoring of a wounded man by a group of peasants. Maino,
Philip IV's art teacher, about whom little is known, in 1625 still subscribed
to the forms of the early Caravaggio which he probably knew in the Lombard phase or the early Roman period. Aside from the importance of its
presence for the young Velázquez, this stupendous scene by Maino has its
own merits. It relates him to the brothers LeNain, and is an exceptionally
true mixture of direct popular spontaneity, limpid forms and closed volu-
metrics, with a rigorous composition of blocks on transverse lines which is
also a heritage from Caravaggio, but here more affable and intimate.

JUSEPE DE RIBERA. *Jacob's Ladder.* *p. 74*
Executed in Naples in the artist's maturity, *Jacob's Ladder* still reveals
Ribera's Caravaggesque training with Ribalta and his direct study of Caravaggio in Rome. As in other paintings in which the formula prevails, Ribera
simplifies figure and composition. He proceeds in terms of strong contrast
in disposition as well as color, with a tendency to reduce the colors to two.

JUSEPE DE RIBERA
(LO SPAGNOLETTO)
Born in Játiva (Valencia), baptized in 1591;
in Italy from 1616; died in Naples, 1652.
Jacob's Ladder (1639)
Oil on canvas; 5'10 1/2" × 7'8". Signed and
dated. Provenance: La Granja (1746) and
the Academia de San Fernando (1827).

JUSEPE DE RIBERA
Aesop
Oil on canvas; 3'10 1/2" × 3'1".
From the Escorial.

JUSEPE DE RIBERA
The Martyrdom of St. Bartholomew
Oil on canvas; 7'8" × 7'8". Signed in lower
right corner and dated 1630 (1639?). From
the Alcazar, Madrid (1666), and the dressing room of the Royal Palace, Madrid
(1794).

This creates a dramatic understatement. And the forms are seen under a
violent illumination that throws the features into exaggerated relief, em-
phasizing their physical realism — which Ribera evidently relished.

JUSEPE DE RIBERA. *Aesop.*
Aesop is an exemplary work of the master who was famous for his figures
of saints, ancient philosophers and mythological heroes, whom he exalted
in terms of a realism that was descriptive and readily comprehensible. His
personages are not "beautiful," but harshly characterized, and the figures
emerge abruptly from their backgrounds under a raking illumination from
one side. Often the result is more spectacular than profound.

JUSEPE DE RIBERA. *The Martyrdom of St. Bartholomew.*
It is one of Ribera's most committed paintings, a rare instance of his pictorial qualities in their full range. There may be a desire to display "academic" skill in the composition that ramifies in various directions from the
central axis of the stake, as well as in the anatomical competence and the
traditionalism of the figure bending forward. The marginal episodes, such
as the spectators to the right, and especially the woman on the lower left,
are incisive and subtle passages, and have more penetrating imaginative
and human emotion than the thunderous central scene.

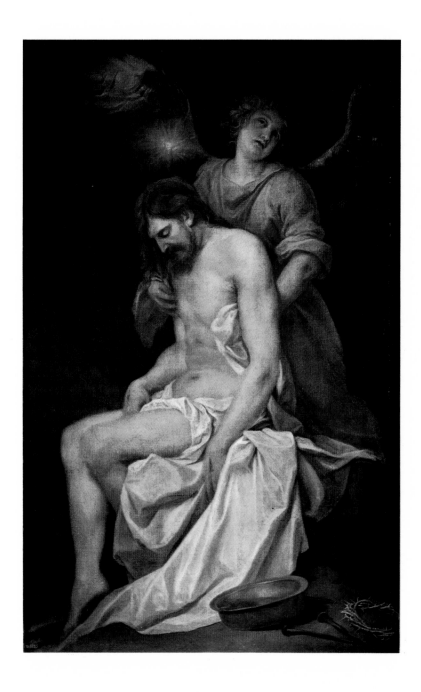

ALONSO CANO. *The Dead Christ Supported by an Angel.*
Variation that may be dated around 1645 of a theme treated several times, in which the Italian and Venetian elements are apparent, as against the artist's first orientation toward Herrera and Caravaggio. Compared to other works of this phase (exemplified by a painting of the beginning of Cano's Madrid period, *Miracle of the Well,* also in the Prado), here we see an attraction to Rubens in the loaded brushwork and the tawny whipped-up color, as well as in the strongly contrasted drama of light and shade.

ALONSO CANO
Granada 1601; in Madrid from 1637 to 1651; died in Granada, 1667.
The Dead Christ Supported by an Angel. Oil on canvas; 4′6″ × 3′3 3/4″.
Signed *"Alo y Cano."*

CLAUDIO COELLO. *The Triumph of St. Augustine.*
76 In this youthful work, Coello departs from Francisco Rizi's teaching and

CLAUDIO COELLO
Madrid 1642 — Madrid 1693
Triumph of St. Augustine (1664)
Oil on canvas; 8′11″ × 6′8″.
Signed and dated.
From the convent of the Augustinians
of Alcalá de Henares (1836);
then in the Museo de la Trinidad.

submits to Roman influences, especially from Pietro da Cortona and Ba-
ciccia. This is accompanied by a strong sympathy for Rubens that extends
to iconographic choices and classical references. In the large terraced landscape, however, an allusion to Poussin's landscape may be noted. His taste
was for sumptuousness and excitement; the spectacle is imposing, with its
radiating lines in the group of flying figures. Coello returned to these visual
effects and compositional bravura after 1685 in the scenes for the Escorial;
they are also imposing scenic compositions, but with intimate passages
developed within a more subtle and contained rendering, though the painting is still opulent and splendid. The art of Cano, Coello and others shows
how despite Velázquez's activity there existed in Spain different cultural ori-
entations, toward Italy, Rubens and other sources.

FRANCISCO ZURBARAN
Still-life
Oil on canvas; 18″ × 33″. Gift of
Francisco A. Cambó, 1940.

FRANCISCO ZURBARAN
Fuente de Cantos (Badajoz) 1598;
was living in Madrid in 1664.
St. Casilda (ca. 1640)
Oil on canvas; 6′3/4″ × 2′11 1/2″
From the Royal Palace, Madrid (1814).

FRANCISCO ZURBARAN. *St. Casilda.*

Painted around 1640, this figure is certainly a portrait (like others belonging to various series of saints). It reveals the Caravaggesque formation of Zurbaran's style: a sculptural simplification of the figures placed without any distracting details against solid backgrounds; side lighting that crystallizes the forms; sumptuous garments of shot silk, in vivid and contrasting colors, which multiply the tonalities into great cascades of crackling color. The color tends to resolve into geometric forms, responding to the volumetric severity of these large, dominating apparitions. They are set apart by their stamp of distant and strict being — secular idols, images of a society closed in its role, ceremonials and rites of supremacy.

FRANCISCO ZURBARAN. *Still-life.*

Like other still-lifes of Zurbaran which are also signed, this painting is first of all an authentic re-interpretation of Caravaggio in one fundamental aspect: the voluntary adoption of a 15th century mode. The four objects (which are found again in other still-lifes by the artist) are placed on a continuous plane that is fixed between two vertical planes — foreground and back-   79

ground — with an extreme reduction of space. The vase and the dishes share the same "pure" volumetric quality, and their composition on the plane corresponds to an equally strict geometry, the lines of which can be obtained by drawing a *plan* of this picture as if it were an architectural elevation. The dishes on the sides are disposed in strict symmetry, as are their shadows. In the center, the left double-handled vase is aligned along the axis of the dishes, while the one to the right is pushed back and placed at an angle whose diagonal, projected toward the spectator, is marked by the

80

FRANCISCO ZURBARAN
The Apostle Peter Appearing to St. Peter Nolasco (1629)
Oil on canvas; 5'10 1/2" × 7'4". Signed and dated in lower center. Painted for the Claustro de la Merced in Seville, with the *Vision of St. Peter Nolasco,* which is also in the Prado. Acquired in 1808.

handles. Another oblique direction is marked by the handles of the vase to the right. At the same time there is a delicate, suspended rhythm of balances in the alternation of heights and sizes of the equidistant objects. Mechanical symmetry is avoided and the image is animated by an internal, almost breathing rhythm.

Beneath an apparent simplicity, the artist shows all the depth and awareness of compositional structure, while the unity of the lateral light isolates the forms in an immobility of contemplation that is continually renewed.

FRANCISCO ZURBARAN. *The Apostle Peter Appearing to St. Peter Nolasco*
This work from Zurbaran's maturity is perhaps the most intensely lyrical of those composing his religious cycles. The bare simplicity of the composition reflects the criteria and solutions indicated in such works as *Still-life,* already discussed. Here are only two figures against an immense closed background, and two summary diagonals, one from right to left, toward the crucified Apostle; the other from left to right, formed by his open arms, which provide a rapid penetrating movement. Corresponding to this last movement are the open arms of St. Peter Nolasco in adoration. The situation is like an unexpected explosion, and it is concentrated in a vision caught at its most forceful moment in an indescribable and marvelous instant. Continuing the Caravaggesque mode, simplified forms in pure volumes are revealed by a miraculous beam of light. Leaving aside any traditional models, and interpreting the narrative in a highly individual way, the artist creates the immediate and compelling image of the two figures. He arrests the sharp feeling not so much of an exceptional event as of the impossibility or incredibility of a miracle. This he does in a suspended tension that is established in the descent of the Apostle Peter, with his aura of light, and in the sudden gesture of St. Peter Nolasco, who appears to have just fallen to his knees after having witnessed the incredible descent. The manner of painting almost annuls his presence, at least as a physical or apparent presence in the eyes of the observer; it suggests a precipitous sublimation, a point of transport, of a transfiguring, lyrical, mystical exaltation that is beyond any situation and any time.

DIEGO VELÁZQUEZ DE SILVA. *The Forge of Vulcan.*   *p. 82*
In this canvas of his early maturity, Velázquez still shows his attraction to the compositions and smooth constructions of domestic interiors that have their origin in Caravaggio. To this tradition also belongs the composition with its diagonal counterpoised planes and directional thrusts forward and to the background, all tied together in a solid framework. The axis of the picture is central, with oblique ramifications and displacements in all directions, converging and diverging at the same time, arresting the internal structure at the extremity of connection and equilibrium. The grace and bearing of the anatomically precise nudes, the easy freedom of the gestures, the varying reactions of the personages in the circuit of the mimed dialogue, the changing colors under the daylight and sunny illumination — all show the artist's sensitivity to the style of Rubens, whom he had met in Madrid in 1628. Velázquez, however, does not diverge from his own temperament of earthy   **81**

DIEGO VELÁZQUEZ DE SILVA
Seville 1599; becomes Master in 1620; in
Madrid 1623; in Italy 1629 (worked in
Venice, Rome, Naples); in Madrid from
1631; from 1648 to 1651 in Italy (Milan,
Florence, Parma, Naples, Rome); died in
Madrid, 1660.
The Forge of Vulcan (1630)
Oil on canvas; 7'4" × 9'6 1/4". Painted in
Rome. Acquired by Philip IV in 1634.
Formerly in the Buen Retiro and the Royal
Palace.

fullness and community with the real world; he rejects emotional trans-
ports and bombast of any sort. Even the presence of Apollo crowned with
laurel, his head radiating light, does not alter the familiar character of a
scene in a forge.

DIEGO VELÁZQUEZ DE SILVA. *Portrait of Philip IV*.

Painted between 1652 and 1653 (according to Lopez-Rey), and in any
case before 1655 (when it was engraving by Pedro de Villafranca), this is
the prototype from life of numerous half-length portraits of the King (others are in: London, National Gallery; Cincinnati Museum; Vienna, Kunsthistorisches Museum; Madrid, Marques de Argüeso; Glasgow, Art Gallery;
Leningrad, Hermitage; Madrid, Academia de S. Fernando; Madrid, Istitudo
de Valencia de Don Juan; Edinburgh, National Gallery; Bilbao Museum;
Turin, Galleria Sabauda; Montreal, Van Horne Collection, etc.). It also
served for numerous other full-length portraits of Philip in various poses
and kinds of dress, executed by the school of Velázquez to satisfy the need
for likenesses of the sovereign in offices, embassies and courts. These works
are generally on a high technical level, but lack the burning interior quality that characterizes the painting by the artist's own hand. Its execution is
extremely rapid and generalized, done in a few moments, and mainly concentrated on the head — surrounded by an even dark grey ground — but
also stressed in the white collar and the very simple black silk garment. The
imperious and at the same time perturbed face of the king — who has been
posed to show his regality — is caught in a moment that permits an inner
uncertainty, a diffident timidity, a defensive haughtiness to come through.
The artist has caught these traits by an intuitive sounding of the depths of

DIEGO VELÁZQUEZ DE SILVA
Portrait of Philip IV (1655–1660)
Oil on canvas; 27 1/4" × 22". Donated by
Ferdinand VII, King of Spain,
to the Academia de San Fernando (1816);
in the Prado in 1827.

his subject, which do not appear in the official portraits. The latter have nothing of the hidden penetration of the Spanish ruler's character, and reveal mainly or only his pride, without the psychological complications.

DIEGO VELÁZQUEZ DE SILVA
The Surrender of Breda (1634–1635)
Oil on canvas; 10'1" × 12'. Formerly in the Royal Palace of El Buen Retiro (1635), then in the New Royal Palace (1772); in the Prado since 1819. Executed in 1634–1635 to commemorate the surrender of Breda: Justin of Nassau handed over the keys of the fortress to General Ambrogio Spinola on June 5, 1625.

DIEGO VELÁZQUEZ DE SILVA.   *The Surrender of Breda.*

It is one of the most important and problematical works of Velázquez. Despite the probable existence of preliminary drawings (for example, in the National Library, Madrid), the canvas underwent a very complicated process of development in successive stages, as X-rays have revealed (changes in the position of the horse, the central group, the position of the lances seen against the plain and the cloudy sky, etc.). The artist's own interest in this masterpiece is shown by his inclusion, on the far right, of a self-portrait. The surface is divided into four parts in a sensitive proportional modulation that intensifies the general dynamic rhythm. Against this rectangular division, around the central group of Nassau and Spinola, there are two curved banks of figures (with the big horse that is turning away): the general staff and the soldiers. Beyond them is the encampment with other lancers sketched in, and in the distance the city and its burning fortifications in the plain that extends to the distant horizon. All the figures are powerfully individualized portraits; the atmosphere is that of an action-camera shot, with everything caught in motion. It is a sunny day; the scene is inundated with vivid transparent colors contrasting with the stupendous lances seen against the light, the halbards to the left, the moving shadows on the ground and the kaleidoscope of parade uniforms. There is neither rhetoric nor Spanish hauteur in this work; indeed, considering the time, it is a sort of calm and good-natured timbre that one registers, in part because Velázquez reduced but did not eliminate the original embrace of the victor and the vanquished.

DIEGO VELÁZQUEZ DE SILVA.   *The Conde-duque de Olivares on Horseback.*   *p. 86*

The picture commemorates the political author of Philip IV's victories (in the background on the left — not visible in the detail reproduced here —

DIEGO VELÁZQUEZ DE SILVA
*The Conde-Duque de Olivares
on Horseback* (ca. 1634)
(Don Gaspar de Guzman)
Oil on canvas; 10'2 1/2" × 7'10 1/2". Detail
of the equestrian portrait. Formerly the property of the subject's family, it was acquired
in 1769 by Charles III from the Marques de
Ensenada. In the Royal Palace from 1772;
in the Prado since 1819.

there is an infantry battle). The rearing horse, in the classical and human-
ist tradition, and the commanding pose of the figure, as in other equestrian
portraits, are conventions imposed by the theme. But in carrying it out the
artist transformed and individualized its character. Starting from the hind-
legs of the horse, and passing through the sword, arm and the baton of
command, a rapid zigzag is traced, which sums up the broken movement
of the figure and the axis of the entire picture, from below to above and
from one end to the other; and mobilizes it completely, aided by all the
other movements and swerves (for instance, the divergence between horse
and rider). A feeling of motion animates every phase and every point and
calls for the landscape that is dramatically rich in changes in level and in
raking light and shade, as well as for the sky full of tumultuous clouds, torn
by luminous breaks, and the wild tree bursting with leaves and branches.
The smoking battle adds a sharp, even tragic note to the breathless action
of the composition, which is coherently accompanied by bursts of color and
by the broken and unexpected patterns of brushwork.

DIEGO VELÁZQUEZ DE SILVA
Prince Balthasar Carlos on Horseback
(1634–1635). Oil on canvas; 6′10 1/4″ ×
5′8″. Painted for El Buen Retiro, where it
hung with the equestrian portraits of Philip
IV (Prado, No. 1178) and Queen Isabella
(Prado, No. 1179). Subsequently it was in
the New Palace (1734–1814); then in the
Prado from 1819.

DIEGO VELÁZQUEZ DE SILVA. *Prince Balthasar Carlos on Horseback.*
Painted between 1634 and 1635, the composition is intended to be immediately and swiftly perceived. There is the general diagonal disposition from
lower right to upper left, and the dynamic reversed curves of the horse; and
in the middle the young prince in ceremonial dress: star shaped with rays
projecting to the horse's mane, harness and tail. The whole explodes against
the oblique hollow of a steep-sided valley, and in the distance a receding
mountain widens the background that fans out under a corruscating sky,
where grey and white clouds pile on top of one another. The stylistic themes
are an assembly of headlong, fugitive motives, made concrete by the brushwork. This is divided, directed, flying and sometimes (as in many other
paintings by the master) reaching the point of broken impastos, thrown directly on the canvas for passionate, accidental effects.

DIEGO VELÁZQUEZ DE SILVA. *Prince Balthasar Carlos in Hunting Dress, with Two Dogs.*

The composition is learned, but simple. Restricted above by the branches of an oak tree, in the lower part of the canvas the figure of the prince and his arquebus is composed in an angular form directed upwards, while the big dog to the left closes off the figure and encircles it. This simple composition, however, is related to a double diagonal directed toward the background to the right and the tree trunk; and in correspondence there are all the levels of the distant landscape divided by valleys and slanting ridges. With a perceptible release, the figure of the prince arrests this falling movement, as if it had energetically overcome some opposing force. In this case, too, the work has the immediate appearance of splendid representation affirming the majesty of kings; but going beyond the required theme, the artist has made the painting into a locus of forces just subdued, of momentary equilibrium between intense pulls, expressing a tension shown throughout, from the format to the manner of painting, which is extraordinarily rich in flowing color and contrasts. Also unusual is how the figures are cut so that they seem taut and compressed at the same time. Abandoning traditional ideas of completeness, the artist crops them (see the dog at the right) as if they had been unexpectedly seen and recorded, a kind of vision that will be understood and taken up by the great French Impressionists, beginning with Manet, to express the instantaneous look of modernity.

DIEGO VELÁZQUEZ DE SILVA. *The Royal Family (Las Meninas).*

The personages are seen in a room in the royal palace with identifiable paintings on the walls — *Apollo and Pan,* school of Rubens; copy of a Jordaens by Mazo, both today in the Prado. Although a little scant of color in the upper part, it is evident how the composition is committed to the influx of light in the "proscenium" and from the background, in a contrast that is barely resolved by the play of perspective: an oblique quadrangle in the foreground, the diagonally placed canvas, the background with its mirrored figures and openings against the light. It is an intimate room. Royalty is out of the picture and participates only by reflection, without altering the gentle, fresh atmosphere of the scene. Velázquez removed every restriction that might have obliged him to alter the tone of everyday life, it might be anyone's life, to that of the court's rituals. In fact, the artist himself assumes the part of the protagonist, with his dominating position and his look expressing a tranquil self-awareness. The scene of homage to the Infanta, through its dwarfs, its modest household members and its faithful dog, is expressed in one of Velázquez's most delicate, refined and vibrant compositions — light in tone and application, with agile passages, contained, pearly touches and in general a supreme expression of expansive affection.

DIEGO VELÁZQUEZ DE SILVA. *The Fable of Arachne (Las Hilanderas).*

p. 90

Painted between 1644 and 1648, the picture represents a scene in Juan Alvarez's tapestry and carpet workshop in Madrid. In the background hangs a tapestry with a representation of Ariadne, in which Veronese motives appear. The mythological title, attested by ancient sources, is valid only for

DIEGO VELÁZQUEZ DE SILVA
Prince Balthasar Carlos in Hunting Dress, with Two Dogs (1635–1636). Oil on canvas; 6′3″ × 3′4 1/2″. The inscription *"Anno aetatis suae VI"* (i.e., aged 6) dates the painting at the end of 1635 or 1636. Restored. Originally there were three dogs (X-ray).

DIEGO VELÁZQUEZ DE SILVA
The Royal Family (Las Meninas or "The Maids of Honor") (1656) Oil on canvas; 10′5″ × 9′1″. Restored in 1735. The painting underwent modifications during execution, as shown by X-ray. Velázquez is seen painting the portraits of Philip IV and Queen Mariana, who are reflected in the mirror, in the presence of the Infanta Doña Margarita, two maids of honor, two attendants, two dwarfs and the Marshal of the Palace (at the door in the background). All the figures have been identified by name.

the tapestry; for the picture as a whole the title of *Las Hilanderas,* the *Tapestry Weavers* (caught at their work in the textile factory), is more justified. Here, too, the over-all composition is of an extreme simplicity: two diagonal lateral wings, lighted in contrast to the shadowed background; in the center a triangular figure against the light, contrasting with the background illuminated by a vivid blade of sunlight; stepped planes moving in alternate lateral jumps toward the background. The scene is a striking closeup. As in the master's last period, and through the impulse derived from his Italian visits, Velázquez, without abandoning his Caravaggesque compositions of linked masses and dialectics of light and dark, is more and more attracted to the pictorial freedom of the Venetians. He is taken by their direct impasto, quivering brushwork, the charm of a dense, warm atmosphere rendered by nuances and reflections. The approach permits an improbable perspective (elsewhere the perspective is strict and measured) to obtain a more intimate movement on all sides — the weavers and the women — with the pulsating effects of light which gives a vitally cheerful movement to the

DIEGO VELÁZQUEZ DE SILVA
The Fable of Arachne
(*Las Hilanderas*) (1644–1648)
Oil on canvas; 7'3" × 9'6" (originally, without the additions, 5'6 1/2" × 8'2"). In 1664 in the collection of Don Pedro de Arce; acquired by Philip V; in the Alcazar (1734), then in the Palacio del Buen Retiro and the New Palace (1772); in the Prado since 1819. Restored after the fire in the Royal Palace in 1734. The 18th century additions include the upper part with the arch, the completion of the figures, the door and the curtain at the sides. Our illustration shows the size of the original.

DIEGO VELÁZQUEZ DE SILVA
Villa Medici in Rome (1630)
Oil on canvas; 17 1/4″ × 15″. In the
Alcazar, Madrid (1666), then in
El Buen Retiro (1772); in the Prado
from 1819.

scene. Here are seen some of the most exceptional and original renderings of movement, as in the hand of the girl on the right, which is multiplied to indicate its gesture, and in other parts that are veiled or caught in action, like the spinning wheel.

DIEGO VELÁZQUEZ DE SILVA. *Villa Medici in Rome*.
This rare landscape was painted in the summer of 1630, when Velázquez lived in the Villa Medici, Rome, copying ancient statues (note the *Sleeping Ariadne* in the background), according to Pacheco. Dated by some scholars 1650–51, it is more probably the precedent for works executed around 1635 (see the background of the *Surrender of Breda*). It may be identified as one of the four small landscapes (of which three are in the Prado) acquired for the King in 1634 by Villanueva. Although the symmetrical disposition, centered on the arch in the background, connects the painting with the Venetian tradition, especially with Paolo Veronese, in one aspect

it reveals itself as an ancestor of modern landscape. The protagonist of the canvas, in fact, is the filtering of light through the trees to the figures, the architecture and the ground. A momentary, passing "impression," an instant of luminous vibration, is caught among the infinite changes of color and summer warmth in the quiet of a midday hour. Between artist and landscape a reciprocity and intimate continuity of relationship are established, by which one seems to penetrate the other in a conjunction that exalts the poetry of a moment.

DIEGO VELÁZQUEZ DE SILVA. *Don Diego de Acedo.*
The dwarf is represented in his function as secretary of the Council of the Signet, or Privy Seal. The figure and the books, papers and inkwell stand out undisturbed by the landscape background, with its threatening sky above a broken line of distant mountains. By setting him in a grandiose tri-

DIEGO VELÁZQUEZ DE SILVA
Pablo de Valladolid
Oil on canvas; 6'10 1/2" × 4'1/2". The
court jester's life between 1632 and 1648 is
documented. In the Palacio Real del Buen
Retiro (1701), then in the New Palace
(1772–1814), the Academia de San Fernando (1816–1827) and the Prado (1827).
Some restoration.

angular composition, Velázquez has made of his deformed subject a hero
(besides, Don Diego was wounded at Molina in 1643, in the attempted as-
sassination of Olivares), austere and pensive in his chaste garb, expressive
of a penetrating and inquiring humanity. The still-life also elevates the subject, the intact whiteness of the books making a vigorous but contained contrast with the black hat and garments.

DIEGO VELÁZQUEZ DE SILVA. *Pablo de Valladolid.*
The portrait is dated around 1635 and represents, after the *Calabazas,* a
moment of fundamental importance in Velázquez's work. The large figure,
painted black on black, is set against a silver grey ground more or less animated by its own light, which flashes in the area between the feet and the
cast shadows, and in the right margin of the picture, contrasting with the   93

black suit and cape. Almost as if rediscovering the pure relationship of body and space defined by shadows, the artist has eliminated all definite limits, and only by indicating the projection of the shadows, has conferred on the composition a character as vehement as an apparition, at the same time establishing a solid architectonic balance. The result was not easy to attain, as is indicated by the numerous afterthoughts or *pentimenti* that are seen especially in the lower part of the picture, where the static structure, obtained by means of a jet of light, achieves its maximum intensity. Several other works of Velázquez — the portrait of Admiral Pareja, and those of the jesters Morra and Barbarroja — share in this search for an "environmental fusion" (Camon Aznar), in which the data of experience are transformed into an interior vision. It is an affirmation of the artist's conception according to which every object or being is an actor in the "theater of the world," as Calderon put it. Everyone's identity must be preserved, in artistic form, in a choral series of "portraits" that make up the infinitely animated universe.

DIEGO VELÁZQUEZ DE SILVA. *Portrait of the Jester Called "Don Juan of Austria."*

In this life-size figure, Velázquez again followed a rigorous standard of perspective. In the space formed by the floor and the wall in the background (open to the right on the scene of a naval battle), the artist traces with "still-life" elements — arquebus, cuirass, helmet, cannon balls — an oblique cross system. At the center of the cross, and linked to it by the angular arrangement of the feet and legs, rises the figure of the court jester in ceremonial dress. It is interesting to note how the cane makes a compass shape with the arquebus on the ground, and how the arms point toward the right-hand corner, which is raised by the helmet. The splendor of the colors, of opulent blacks and crimsons, and the rippling brushwork full of animation and unexpected jumps, does not alter the monumentality achieved by the composition, which exalts its subject. At the same time, the character of a simple man decked out in plumes has been preserved.

DIEGO VELÁZQUEZ DE SILVA. *The Infanta Margarita.*

Long confused with that of the Infanta Maria Teresa, this portrait, according to authoritative studies, is considered the last work by the master. Dated around 1660, it was completed by Juan Bautista Martinez del Mazo (died in Madrid in 1667), who reproduced the portrait in his painting of the Velázquez family (now in Vienna). Not easily judged because of repainting, even on the face, this official portrait is executed brilliantly with a broad use of reflections in the silk and gold embroidery of the sumptuous dress. It represents the ceremonial pomp of the Spanish court at its apogee. Lacking, however, are the vibrant transparencies and the lively jets of color — the light upon lights, as it were — that are typical of the best works by the artist's own hand. It is an elevated example of the production to which Velázquez and his students and assistants devoted themselves to meet the needs of the court.

BARTOLOMÉ ESTEBAN MURILLO. *The Immaculate Conception.*

In this late work, it is clear that Murillo looked to Guido Reni for the "sentimental" faces and to van Dyck for technique. The painting, however, is among the most integrated and successful of his last period, with its atmospheric density animated by suffused gleams, and the light figures enveloped in a luminous haze. Never leaving Madrid, Murillo picked up at a distance and through various intermediaries what was going on in contemporary painting, and after an early neo-Caravaggesque period influenced by Ribalta, Ribera and Zurbaran, he turned to Reni, Rubens and van Dyck. His production was vast, alternating works of a marked "realistic" character with others in which the accent of devotion does not concern only the religious themes, but also the manner of painting. Murillo has long been appreciated and famous, even more than his other great contemporaries, for his masterly expression. In works with a strong literary or religious content, his undoubted talent is not always accompanied by the lyric accent that is found in his penetrating portraits or in his intimate representations of ordinary life.

BARTOLOMÉ ESTEBAN MURILLO. *Holy Family (del Pajarito).*

Painted around 1650, it is among the works that still show Murillo close to Zurbaran and Ribera. In this domestic scene the emphasis is on its character as a playful interlude, without any sacred feeling. The composition intelligently adopts the counterpoised blocked-out masses of the Caravaggesque heritage, and the diagonal relationships, which are however attenuated in a composed but fluent dialogue of forms. In this work of his early maturity, Murillo also shows his qualities as an ingratiating designer of scenes keyed to a sentiment between the religious and the commonplace, in an atmosphere of softly indulgent devotion, which is well served by his pictorial skill.

97

BARTOLOMÉ ESTEBAN MURILLO. *Rebecca and Eleazar.*

Typical of Murillo's middle period is the taste for Ribera and the references to Reni. The Biblical scene takes place on a stage immediately presented to the spectator and is developed in the arc of figures around the cylindrical well. The handling of the terra-cotta amphora emphasizes the divergence of directions, and the compositional bridge between Eleazar and the group of women is clear and simple. In the background to the left, in the road in the valley, a caravan waits in sunlight, a device frequent in Murillo. The color, especially in the marginal areas, preserves the smoky contrasts of Ribera, but in the polite, somewhat idealized figures of the women, it is enlivened by pleasingly liquid as well as ringing notes. The high, sometimes conventional, professionalism typical of many of Murillo's works, is surpassed in this calm, intimate and luminous performance.

It is typical of the artist, in this as in other representations of sacred themes (the Mosaic and Christological scenes in La Caridad, Seville, 1670–74), to shift the main interest to genre aspects, refining and rendering affable representations of the contemporary world, especially the peasant's. There is a

BARTOLOMÉ ESTEBAN MURILLO
Rebecca and Eleazar
Oil on canvas; 3'6 1/4″ ×5'7 1/4″. Acquired in Seville by Isabella Farnese in 1733, then in the collection at La Granja (1766); subsequently entered the Prado. Executed around 1650.

sentimental inflection which, declining from an intentionally realistic point of departure toward the crudely pictorial (as in the beggars), would be appreciated by the pastoral Arcadians of the following century.

LUIS EUGENIO MELÉNDEZ. *Still-life with Salmon and Lemon.*
In the reduction and simplification of composed images, Meléndez went back to 17th century Italian and Dutch models of the school of Caravaggio, and shows influences from Velázquez, whom he undoubtedly observed with filial spirit. Thus the single source of light isolates and exalts every object with its own individual coloration, and scans the connection along the diagonal that meets the trihedral disposition of vases at the left. There is no lack of textural observation and sensitive taste for materials, especially in the meat of the salmon, the difference between the vessels, the translucent lemon peel. The immobile composition has authority and a silent density. It has been pondered and animated in terms of light and color and has a lasting, intense fascination. In pictures like this, Meléndez passed over the recent fashion for the Flemish taste or for Mario dei Fiori, as seen in such immediate precedents as the work of Juan de Arellano or Pérez, and returned to the models of Sanchez Cotan, Juan de Espinosa, Pedro de Camprobin and other artists of the first half of the 17th century.

LUIS EUGENIO MELÉNDEZ
Naples 1716; in Madrid from 1717; died in Madrid, 1780.
Still-life with Salmon and Lemon
Oil on canvas; 16 1/2″ × 28 3/4″. Signed on the edge of the table: *"L. Mz DºISº Pr Ano 1772." Painted for Aranjuez, with a series of* other canvases also in the Prado.

FRANCISCO DE GOYA Y LUCIENTES
Fuendetodos 1746; in Madrid 1763; in Italy ca. 1770, Rome 1771; Madrid 1773; Painter to the King 1786 and *Pintór de Camera* in 1789; in 1819 at *Quinta del Sordo;* exile in Bordeaux from 1824; died in Bordeaux, 1828.

The Parasol
Oil on canvas; 3′5″ × 4′11 3/4″. Tapestry cartoon for an over-door in the dining room of El Pardo; executed on August 12, 1777.

FRANCISCO DE GOYA Y LUCIENTES. *The Parasol.*

By a wall, the elegant young Spanish girl sits in the sun, from which a *Maja* shades her with a green umbrella. With the tapestry cartoons of the same series, ordered from him by Charles III, this represents the first emergence of Goya's personality as a painter, reflecting in theme and background of woods and brush the French taste brought to Madrid by Houasse and even more the clear, fluent techniques of Giaquinto. It is a happy, sunny scene, with a gradation of colors which recalls the range of Tiepolo, especially in the abrupt dips in the blacks. In this and succeeding paintings, Goya's imagination is seen as luminously serene, in a climate without clouds or doubt, torment or pain; a manifestation of joy in life and a paean to its fullness and beauty.

FRANCISCO DE GOYA Y LUCIENTES. *Man Drinking.*

This is another scene of genre or Spanish manners, executed for the same series, and conceived and carried out by Goya in terms of contrasts between the various canvases. Compared to the preceding painting, this one has a more dramatic tone. Against a background sky that is equally clouded and vaporous stand the figures, at the edge of a wood traversed by rays of light that animate the colors. In theme there is recourse to Dutch genre scenes, but the technique is liquid, thin, pearly, with a fanciful and rich choice of colors that are concentrated in full sunlight, especially on the three figures of the *Majas* to the right.

FRANCISCO DE GOYA Y LUCIENTES
Man Drinking
Oil on canvas; 3'6" × 4'11 1/2".
Tapestry cartoon for an over-door in
the dining room of El Pardo;
executed on August 12, 1777.

101

FRANCISCO DE GOYA Y LUCIENTES
The Snowfall
Oil on canvas; 9'1/4" × 9'7 1/2". Cartoon
for a tapestry (which has been preserved),
painted for the El Pardo series at the end of
1786 or the beginning of 1787; sketch
(12 1/2" × 13") in the Silberman collection,
New York.

FRANCISCO DE GOYA Y LUCIENTES. *The Snowfall.*

Some hunters and a dog followed by a mule loaded with a dead boar are crossing a valley during a snowfall and a blizzard that is bending the bare tree. Goya — with some suggestion of satisfied bravura — has played up the general effect of the whites of the snow under the heavy grey sky, manipulating with careful calculation the thickening surfaces and the subtle chromatic variations. The group, from the man in front with the gun to the mule, has a forward movement that expands against the background with its leveled surfaces. In the figures, especially the two to the left, the artist works with extreme freedom of technique, fractioning the brushstrokes to a degree of pointillism.

FRANCISCO DE GOYA Y LUCIENTES. *The Flower Women.*

With the other canvases of the same series, this one represents a moment of return, but with a more mature and personal command of pictorial language. The atmosphere is bright, the sun glorious, the countryside and the hill already warm in the full springtime. The festive figures are caught exchanging flowers, while the countryman holds a baby rabbit in his hand. The cycle to which this work belongs is developed predominantly in this key of effusion and enjoyment of life. There are however episodes, such as the *Injured Mason,* in a more severe and reflective tone, denser in composition, less relaxed in technique, with unexpected and impassioned passages.

FRANCISCO DE GOYA Y LUCIENTES
The Flower Women
Oil on canvas; 9'1 1/4" × 6'4". Painted after
June 29, 1786, for the "Dormitorio de los
Infantes Don Gabriel y Doña Maria Ana
Victoria" in the Escorial, where the tapestry
is preserved. A reduced version made by the
artist for Alameda de Osuna is today in the
Montellano collection, Madrid.

FRANCISCO DE GOYA Y LUCIENTES
Josefa Bayeu de Goya
Oil on canvas; 32″ × 22″. The identification
of the subject is traditional (she married
Goya in 1773, died in 1812). Acquired from
the Museo de la Trinidad in 1866.

FRANCISCO DE GOYAS Y LUCIENTES. *Josefa Bayeu de Goya.*
Composed according to a simple triangular distribution, the seated half-
length figure is mantled in tulle and has gold-embroidered sleeves. According to most critics the painting dates from 1798. It presents a moment of
sedate intimacy on the part of the artist, even if the forms do not lose their
pulsating animation. It is contained within a subtle range and technique,
concentrating on the meditative face and expression. The angular format is
traditional, but confers a tranquil, communicative quality on the figure. It
evidently was chosen so as to stay within a subdued, low-voiced key that
would not permit any distractions.

FRANCISCO DE GOYA Y LUCIENTES
San Isidro's Hermitage on His Feast Day
Oil on canvas; 16 1/2″ × 17 1/4″. Related,
like the *Meadow of San Isidro,* to a tapestry
cartoon on which Goya was working in May,
1788; paid for by the Duque de Osuna in
1799; Fernandez-Duran bequest (1930).

FRANCISCO DE GOYA Y LUCIENTES. *San Isidro's Hermitage on His Feast Day.*

This sketch, like many others of the same period, continuing the first phase of the artist's work, shows the growth of a more dramatic impetus, whose stimulus is to be found as much in Magnasco as in Watteau. The layout emphasizes his development; contrasts in size increase, points of view are raised or lowered, light and shade are more clashing, the groups near and distant are separated by spatial leaps. The technique is also more urgent and fragmented, richer in clear-cut shadows; the brushwork is biting and immediate, defining and accenting with a few essential touches, swift flicks that break and agitate the silken ground of the colors.

FRANCISCO DE GOYA Y LUCIENTES. *The Nude Maja. pp. 106–107*
On a functional green ottoman, the *Maja,* disposed along a simple diagonal, lies on silken cushions and finely worked sheets; her expression is more naked than her beautiful body. It is one of the most disconcerting images in all art, in which the exaltation of life in the feminine being is triumphant. Goya completely identifies himself with this celebration of beauty, which is not abstract nor an ideal canon, but an enthusiastic participation. The resplendent body lives in the embrace of the light, which seems to love her, as in the ancient myth. The light is a mobile element in the room, and it creates hollows of secret shadow and unexpected radiance; it dazzles and skims, slips along the body and the textures of cloth, shines with palpita-

Pages 106–107:

FRANCISCO DE GOYA Y LUCIENTES
The Nude Maja
Oil on canvas; 3′2 1/4″ × 6′3″. Companion piece to the following painting, and like it painted during the years 1797–1798. In the inventory of its owner, the royal favorite Godoy, the two figures are called "Gypsies." Formerly in the Academia de San Fernando; in the Prado since 1901. Despite their strong resemblances and the identical pose, perhaps two different models were employed.

tions and respirations — forming an indescribable flow of satisfied and exuberant life. This creation of Goya's, though it may have distant ancestors from Titian to Correggio, is disconcertingly new. In climate and in form it established the model by a projection — without pretexts or screens — of the sensibility and vision of an artist, which will be understood by artists of the following century, especially the French.

FRANCISCO DE GOYA Y LUCIENTES
The Clothed Maja
Oil on canvas; 3′1″ × 6′3″.
Same circumstances and date as
the preceding painting.

FRANCISCO DE GOYA Y LUCIENTES. *The Clothed Maja.*
The Clothed Maja repeats the composition of the preceding work, both in the diagonal and in the crescent arc formed by the arms behind the head. There are considerable differences however in the general harmony and color. The moment chosen is toward evening; the lights and shadows are more marked and intense, the grounds more golden and transparent. The body has less the effect of effusing an aura, but is strongly stated in the splendor of a white dress which takes the full impact of the light. Although apparently identical, the figure's pose is different from that of the nude *Maja;* it is more relaxed — not slightly contracted — and rests on the calves rather than the feet, which project over the edge of the divan. Repose is complete, without the slight tension, the waiting air, of the nude. The position appears to be drawn farther back, with no cushion behind the head. It does not have the nude's tendency to turn toward the spectator; it is more comfortably settled, in a different equilibrium. The two subtly suggested moments explain the different positions of the heads — even though the more extended, inviting attitude of the nude's has been charged, through misunderstanding, with being anatomically incorrect.

FRANCISCO DE GOYA Y LUCIENTES. *The Family of Charles IV.*
The 13 figures (and the self-portrait of the painter in the background to the left) are placed, as if on an ideal checkerboard, in "wings" that are bal-

FRANCISCO DE GOYA Y LUCIENTES
The Family of Charles IV
Oil on canvas; 9'2 1/4" × 11'1/4". Painted
at Aranjuez in the spring of 1808, after several individual portraits and sketches, also in
the Prado. All the subjects except two have
been identified. In 1814 it was in the Royal
Palace, Madrid.

anced with respect to Queen Maria Luisa and the King, but following diagonal axes and disposed in uneven masses. A movement and displacement are
thus created in the composition, which is accentuated by the almost revolv-
ing central group; while the background is also sectioned unequally by the
canvas hanging on the wall. The magnificence of the ceremonial costumes
is almost vulgar; they glitter with silks, gold and silver embroidery and
masses of bejeweled and beribboned decorations. Cast shadows and thick
hollows of shadow form a lowering, clouded atmosphere, an unquiet and
in places anxious climate, reflected in the poses of the figures, some of which
have been caught in attentive and others in distracted attitudes. It is a group
portrait of royal personages who, perhaps because of the burning vitality
they emanate, forgave the artist his aggressive exposure of their characters.
Goya's insight borders on cruelty as he parades the series of masks, some

109

of which (the old Maria Josefa, the Queen) are carried boldly close to the grotesque. In all the figures there is something hooked, occasionally feral, that reveals vitality but even more the repressed or inarticulate violence of weak aristocratic temperaments — the vices of a decadent race.

FRANCISCO DE GOYA Y LUCIENTES. *The Second of May 1808.*
The scene represents the assault of the people of Madrid on Napoleon's Mameluke horsemen and dragoons. In the ferocity of the mob there was a seeming renewal of Spain's historical conflict with the Moors, just as there would be again against the Moroccans 125 years after 1808. In the city square, amid clouds of smoke, the Madrid partisans attack the forces of repression without quarter; the latter desperately defend themselves against knives and daggers and point-blank gunshots. The composition appears to begin outside the picture, to the left, and brakes and diverts to the right (interrupted here, too), utilizing the figures of the running horses, terrified by the wheeling sabres, and of the unhorsed Mameluke who is being stabbed.

FRANCISCO DE GOYA Y LUCIENTES
The Second of May, 1808
Oil on canvas; 8'9" × 11'3 1/2". With the following companion canvas, it was ordered by the King, on March 9, 1814, to commemorate the Madrid insurrection against Napoleon. Formerly in the reserves (1834), it has been in the museum proper since 1936. While being transported from Valencia to Catalonia, both canvases were damaged, but have been subsequently restored.

The scene leaves aside any traditional composition and is presented as an immediate, momentary vision of a violent event, caught and stopped at a climactic instant. The truncated mode of composing the action became a tradition of its own, especially in the following century in France. The color is contrasting, broken, often sketchy and spasmodic, in keeping with the general precipitous movement. The faces are summary and fugitive. The horses are massively built and accentuate with their heavy galloping forms the multiplication of converging movements which are directed toward the group under assault. War aroused Goya's imagination and passionate feelings of humanity. Here he was fascinated by a vision of naked ferocity and produced one of the most burningly emotional works in the history of painting.

FRANCISCO DE GOYA Y LUCIENTES
The Third of May, 1808
Oil on canvas; 8'9" × 11'3 1/2". Detail
Same vicissitudes as
The Second of May, 1808.

FRANCISCO DE GOYA Y LUCIENTES.   *The Third of May 1808.*
The scene represents an episode in the reprisals of the French troops. A mass execution is taking place. Three dead bodies lie in the blood; a monk   111

and five men on the left are receiving the volley. Near them, coming up along the wall illuminated by a lantern, is another file of the condemned. It is night; against the dark sky, a church and some houses; in the foreground, circled with penetrating light and cast shadows, the brutal, merciless execution. Our attention is attracted by the figure of the condemned man in a white shirt with his arms raised who is defying the killers, bent over and absorbed in taking aim, while the monk prays and other men make despairing gestures. It is an evocation terrible in its incisiveness, almost premonitory of more recent episodes of ferocious and indiscriminate massacre. And certainly, without a great ethical force, a profound intuition of man's barbarism, Goya could not have expressed with such Homeric gravity this supreme moment in which the millennial cult of violence and death is celebrated. His human participation in the event is grasped in the picture's atmosphere of a tragedy that has been suffered. This is not the case in Manet's *Execution of Maximilian,* which was inspired by Goya's work. In Manet's painting a sort of skeptical detachment prevails, with the interest in the pictorial problem serenely dominating all else; a feeling that has no part in this terrible, fulminating epic of modern barbarism.

FRANCISCO DE GOYA Y LUCIENTES
Brawl with Cudgels
Oil on plaster; 4'1/2" × 8'9". Part of the group of paintings with which Goya, from 1820 to 1822, decorated the *Quinta del Sordo,* "House of the Deaf Man," outside Madrid that he had bought in 1819.

FRANCISCO DE GOYA Y LUCIENTES
Self-Portrait
Oil on canvas; 18″ × 13 3/4″. Signed in up-per part: *"Fr. Goya Aragonés. Po el mismo."*
A similar example, dated 1815, is in the Academia de San Fernando. Acquired in 1866 for the Museo de la Trinidad. Gener-ally dated 1817–1819.

FRANCISCO DE GOYA Y LUCIENTES. *Brawl with Cudgels.*
Goya was over 70 years old; he had lived through 20 tragic years of Span-ish history; in such private or "secret" paintings he took up again and de-veloped those "cabinet pictures" of 1794 about which he wrote: "To oc-cupy the imagination mortified by meditating on my ills . . . I set myself to painting a series of pictures in which I have succeeded in making place for observations that are generally absent in commissioned works, where caprices and inventions cannot be developed." This project and its later re-vival mark an historical fact of the highest importance: the transformation of the artist's aims. He no longer receives or executes commissions, but im-poses his own original expression, not only in form but also in theme, ac-cording to his own choice. In these *Quinta del Sordo* (House of the Deaf Man) pictures, Goya used motives from his previous drawings and prints, but he moved towards a basic monochrome in painting, absolutely inde-pendent of any traditional theme and aimed only to pin down the interior images of a tense, tragic, period in his desperately solitary confessions.   113

FRANCISCO DE GOYA Y LUCIENTES. *Self-portrait.* p. 113

In this self-portrait Goya shows an attraction to Rembrandt, in the reduction of colors to whites, blacks, ochres, off-reds and in the concentrated presentation. Swift improvisation marks the execution, which makes concrete a state of mind preoccupied with meditation and inner crisis — an anxious questioning that remains without answers.

FRANCISCO DE GOYA Y LUCIENTES. *The Aquelarre.*

Our detail represents a group of hags and other women listening to the goat dressed as a monk. It is a lacerated image of Goya's reaction — he had been persecuted before his exile — to the forces of reaction that defeated the hopes of enlightenment brought in by the French Revolution. The figures are feral, avidly reaching for blind irrationalism, unleashing elementary and destructive passions. The monochrome tonality, kindled here and there by flashes of color, adds power to this burning expression of despair. In solitude Goya gave vent to an emotionally lucid and suffering confession of the catastrophe of his time.

FRANCISCO DE GOYA Y LUCIENTES
The Aquelarre
Oil on plaster, transferred to canvas;
4'7" × 14'5". Detail of one of the 14 oils
executed by Goya on the walls of
the *Quinta del Sordo*. In the Prado
since 1881.

FRANCISCO DE GOYA Y LUCIENTES. *Saturn Devouring One of His Children.* p. 116

One of Goya's most terrible visions of inhuman violence and of the liberation of destructive instincts, which were the torment of the artist's last dark years. In this case, too, he had recourse to Rembrandt's summary, torn compositions and the brushstrokes sustain the artist in the drastic compression of the image and its impressive emergence from the timeless night. The technique expresses a savage fury of slaughter and self-destruction. Starting from a sunny climate, Goya endured a long interior journey which arrived at these revelations of the savage and ferocious depths of man, where conscience is overcome and reason is annulled.

FRANCISCO DE GOYA Y LUCIENTES
Saturn Devouring One of His Children
Oil on plaster, transferred to canvas;
4'9 1/2" × 2'8 1/2". This painting comes
from the dining room of the *Quinta del
Sordo*.

FLANDERS

ROGIER VAN DER WEYDEN. *Descent from the Cross.*

It marks the moment of the artist's maturity and is one of his most monumental conceptions. The scene, as in contemporaneous sculpture, directly relates to theatrical performances. The space is a narrow stage on which the sculptural figures are compressed in twos — threes at the center — that do not protrude beyond the architectural setting. Walls close off the stage. The ground is rocky and has flowers growing in it. The composition moves from St. John to the Magdalen on the right. In this large curve, the fainting Madonna and the lifeless body of Christ inscribe two big repeating ellipses, moving laterally and arrested above by other curves moving in the opposite direction. This web of agitated motion (to which other associated elements are connected) also has repercussions from front to back in the entangled and embracing figures. The complex thus organized in a narrow space, within a reduced volume, assumes an agitated, dramatic quality through the containment of geometric and volumetric rhythms. This is reinforced by internally connected flows and returns, which require a visual itinerary that is continuous, but rich in breaks and contrasts. To this compositional drama is added the plastic elements of the figures and the drapery — restless and fragmented — as well as the discontinuous rhythm of the distances both

ROGIER VAN DER WEYDEN
Tournai 1399 (?); in the studio of R. Campin in 1427; Master in 1432; in Italy in 1449; died in Brussels, 1464.
Descent from the Cross
Tempera on panel; 18 1/2″ × 13 3/4″. The central part of a triptych (the wings are lost) painted for the Chapel of the Crossbowmen of Louvain in the years 1439–1443; in the Escorial since 1574 (copy in St. Peter's, Louvain; another copy done in 1569 by Michel Coxcie is in the Escorial).

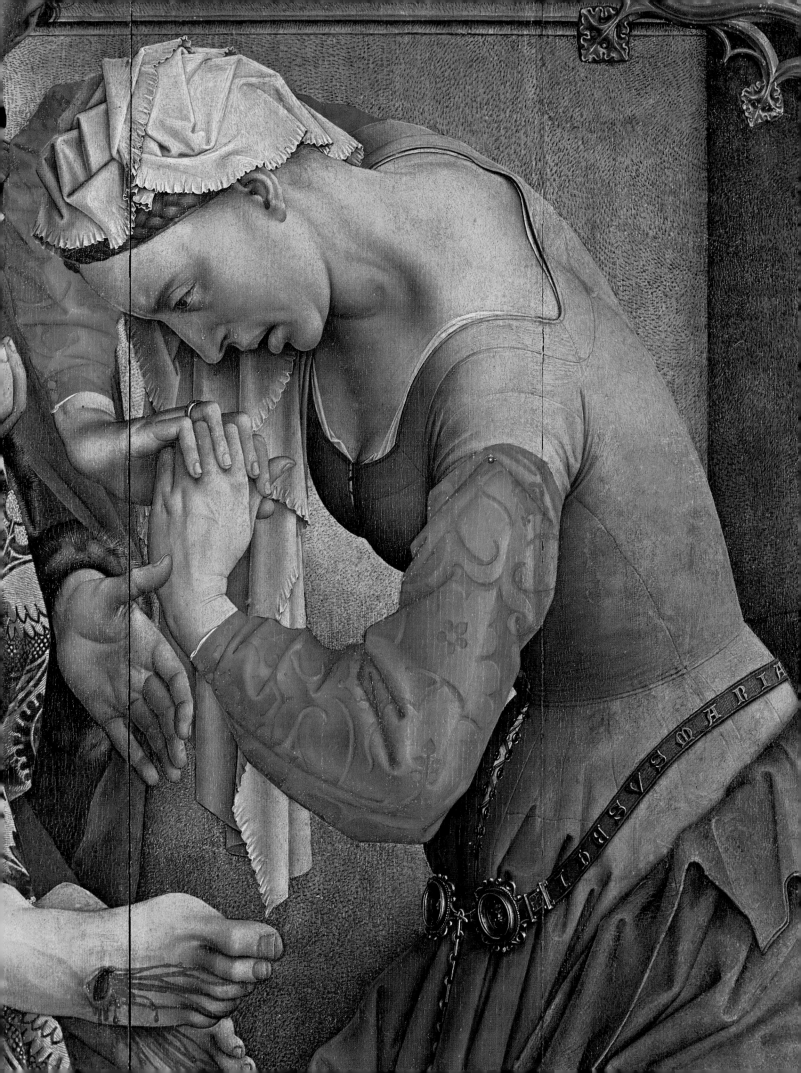

above and below of the intersecting solids and voids. The artist does not spare sumptuous and brilliant notes in the grandiose composition, which achieves by stylistic means a rare power of tragic representation.

ROGIER VAN DER WEYDEN. *Pietà.*

One of many examples from Rogier's studio, it is datable around 1450 and presupposes the experience acquired during the artist's journey to Italy in 1449–50. This is apparent in the perspective landscape and the cross set obliquely in the direction of the body of Christ — with a suggestion of a compass-form opening the space. Flemish pictorial language prevails in the sacred parts of the composition, blocked out in almost rocky forms, while the foreshortened onlooker is defined in more simplified shapes that are not stripped down and hollowed out like those at the side, with their fragmented, pathetic gestures.

MASTER OF FLÉMALLE. *Annunciation.*   *p. 122*

The composition of the two figures is similar to that of the Mérode Triptych (The Cloisters, Metropolitan Museum). The scene is set in the wing of a Gothic church with cross-vaulted bays on the interior; on the exterior are an apse, a tower with spires and in the background, walls and tower. An angled perspective makes a superb scenic effect in which each figure is given a symmetrical space equivalent on the interior and exterior (the panel has been cut down). The interior of the nave or transept is furnished like a domestic household. The composition has a firm balance of parts in its oblique projection, and the figures correspond to each other in the general rhythm. The artist's main interest lies in the refined construction of the setting and its strong architectural forms, which are rich in light, and in which every detail has been brought alive in a crystalline atmosphere through subtle research and accurate evocation.

MASTER OF FLÉMALLE. *St. John the Baptist with Henry of Werl —*
St. Barbara Reading.   *p. 123*

In this work again the positive interest is in the setting: a veranda where the Franciscan is kneeling and praying at the door (open on the sacred scene in the center), while the convex mirror on the wooden partition reflects the backs of the figures. In the other panel, St. Barbara is seated in front of open shutters on a bench by a fireplace in which a fire is lit. In a splendid translucence, the artist develops a perspective with several vanishing points; those controlling the upper parts create a convergence to the center of the missing central panel, while the others are placed so as to rise vertically, sharpening the distance and — especially in the right-hand panel — creating a wide-angle lens effect that brings out the quality of the space and the assertive volumes of the properties. Each household object has its individuality, is lovingly identified and contemplated, is enhanced by light, or rather the various sources of light, if one notices the intersection of the shadows cast by the sun and by the fire. But a fluttering multiplication of light is everywhere: half-light, shadow, penumbra, each separately characterized to give the scene a lucidly modulated gamut of colors.

MASTER OF FLÉMALLE
(ROBERT CAMPIN)
Annunciation
Tempera on panel; 2′6″ × 2′3 1/2″. Companion piece to the *Marriage of the Virgin,* also in the Prado. Attributed also to the young Rogier van der Weyden and to Jacques Daret, disciple of Campin. The two panels — one acquired by Jacopo Trezzo — came into the Escorial in 1577 and 1584; to the Prado in 1839.

MASTER OF FLÉMALLE
(ROBERT CAMPIN)
St. John the Baptist and Henry of Werl
St. Barbara Reading
Tempera on panels: 39 3/4″ × 18 1/2″. On the *St. John* wing is the inscription: *"Ano milleno c qter et octo hic fecit effigiê depigi mister Hîricus Werlis mgr Colon."* The theologian Werl was in Tournai in 1435 (he died in 1461); these panels are dated 1438. Lateral wings of a triptych (central panel lost).

123

HANS MEMLING.   *Adoration of the Magi.*

Another version of this triptych, with variations, is in the Hospital of St. John in Bruges and is signed and dated 1479; this work is dated by scholars around 1470. As in the triptych for Sir John Donne (1468, at Chatsworth) and in other paintings of the period, Memling conceived the representation in terms of quantities and qualities of light: distant sunlight; shadows and

Right: Detail.

HANS MEMLING
Aschaffenburg circa 1433 — Bruges 1494
Adoration of the Magi (ca. 1470)
(Central panel of a triptych; lateral wings: *Nativity* and *Purification*.)
Tempera on panel; 3'1 1/4" × 4'9" (triptych: 95 × 63, 145, 63). It belonged to Charles V and was formerly in the oratory of Ateca. In the Prado since 1847.

silhouette effects in the middle ground; indoor daylight in foreground. With this range, the artist created an airy narrative rich in incident and imagery. The most inventive episode is that of the ruined church covered with a thatched porch. In front of its aisles open to the countryside and the stumps of its arcades, the sacred drama takes place with ritual solemnity, in accordance with a subtly balanced distribution of figures. An elegant and varied range of color is brought alive by the lighting from the side.

JOACHIM PATINIR
Dinant ca. 1480; in 1515 Master at Antwerp where he died in 1524.
Landscape with the Stygian Lake
(after 1521)
Oil on panel; 2'1" × 3'4 1/2".
From the Escorial

JOACHIM PATINIR. *Landscape with the Stygian Lake.*

The art of this master landscapist is based on a knowledge of Bosch, but also of Dürer and of Leonardo da Vinci, perhaps through the medium of Metsys. Amid groups of high dolomitic rocks, the landscape opens out to distant vistas, like topographical air views, following a Leonardesque norm of perspective in which the near view is chromatically rich and articulate, while the far is progressively blued by the density of the atmosphere. The subject of the painting is clearly a pretext, and the landscape is the hero. Dürer noted in his diary that Patinir was a *gut landschaftsmaler* — a good landscape painter — thus establishing not so much his specialization as his independent orientation. In this work, too, the Elysian Fields; Charon in his boat with the damned soul, in the center; flaming and smoking Tartarus to the right, its entrance guarded by the dog Cerberus — these are only anecdotal elements introduced in a balanced, contrasting mixture that is almost pre-Romantic of a "blessed shore" of hills, woods and rivers, and a fire that spreads its black soot, but cannot alter the fascinating vision of immensity. There is a magic in these natural elements, the deep amorous spell of a flourishing land that appears to have been caught in a moment of fresh and clear dawn, at the awakening of all things in the visible world.

JOACHIM PATINIR. *The Temptation of St. Anthony.*

The inventory of the Escorial made in 1574 carries the statement that the figures are "by the hand of Master Coyntin" (Quentin Metsys, 1466–1530) and the landscape by "Master Joaquin." The collaboration (Patinir collaborated with other painters in various works) is limited to the figures in the foreground and those in the erotic scene at the right, inspired by Bosch. In the female figures, especially the caricatured old one, the reference to Leonardo is clear. Beyond the opulently colored curve shape formed by the temptresses around the hermit-saint, the landscape goes deep into the distance. As in other examples, it is caught while bathed in air that is clean, transparent, as in an interval between downpours; and as it moves to the distant horizon, the landscape reveals masses of trees, prairies, buildings and a basin of reflecting water that branches out into tortuous rivers. It is the "peace after the storm," still dripping from the dark clouds — a respite of calm that opens and expands in the vision.

126

JOACHIM PATINIR
The Temptation of St. Anthony
Oil on panel; 5'1" × 5'8 1/4".
Signed: *"Opus Joachim at . . . nier."*
Formerly in the Escorial (1574).

QUENTIN METSYS
Louvain 1466; in 1491 Master at
Antwerp where he died in 1530.
The Mocking of Christ
Oil on panel; 5'3" × 3'11 1/4".
Lanuza bequest, 1936.
In the Prado since 1940.

QUENTIN METSYS. *The Mocking of Christ.*

This work may be dated around 1510. The composition is meant to be seen
from below, as the panel originally was probably the wing of a triptych
placed high on an altar. Within the complex of traditional references to
earlier Flemish painting, the work shows signs of Italian influence not only
in the unified perspective but in the development of the figures, and especially in the recourse to the caricatural grotesques of Leonardo. These,
however, as in other works by Metsys, are even more exaggerated in their
grimaces and their vulgar or deformed aspects, and create an agitated,
howling scene contrasting with the manifest nobility of Christ and of Pilate,
who is standing beside Him in opulent robes.

BERNARD VAN ORLEY. *Holy Family.*

The artist unites the cults for two painters considered princes at the beginning of the 16th century, Dürer and Raphael, thus confirming his motto:

BERNARD VAN ORLEY
Brussels ca. 1488; in 1516 he superintended
the weaving of the Raphael tapestries; in
1518 he was painter to Margaret of Austria;
died in Brussels, 1542.
Holy Family (1522)
Oil on panel; 2'11 1/4" × 2'5". Signed on the
representation of the scrap of paper: BER.
ORLEIUS/FACIEBAT/AN. 1522. Replica in the
Brussels museum. From the Convento de
Las Huelgas, Medina del Pomar; Bosch be-
quest.

"Let everyone be of his own time." The work has been carefully thought
out: the composition converges on the Madonna in the graduated shapes;
the Italian-style composition has a window framing a landscape. But van
Orley's approach is original, even if his pictorial language comes from historical sources. This is seen in the anecdotal and naturalistic observations
of the numerous details, such as the subtly and accurately indicated basket
of flowers, the fruit, the carpet, the book, the golden crown.

HIERONYMUS BOSCH. *The Hay Wain.*   *p. 130*
The moral and religious key to this allegory of the Church is provided by
the angel who turns to the diaphanous Christ in the clouds. The vehicle of
carnal pleasures, which runs over many sinners on its course, is also the object of desire of many who try to get on board with hooks and ladders, and
it is followed by emperor, kings and princes on horseback. In the center

HIERONYMUS BOSCH
's Hertogenbosch between 1480 and 1512 —
's Hertogenbosch 1561
The Hay Wain (central panel)
Triptych. On the outside of the wings, *Road of Life;* on the inside: *The Earthly Paradise, The Hay Wain* or *Pleasures of the Flesh, Hell.*
Oil on panel; height 4'5" × 17 3/4" the wings. × 100 in the central panel.
Signed *"Iheronimus Bosch"* in Gothic letters.

and in the foreground are episodes alluding to the major vices. In the background, a landscape goes deep into a distant blue. The allegory and subject matter invite attention, and might dominate the interest of the viewer if he does not observe the form in which the representational material is absorbed and resolved. The picture is lucidly composed of three parts in aerial perspective, following Leonardo, and like the next triptych (which is considered to be a little later, because of the absence of traditional pictorial elements), has a tendency toward the crystalline in every form. Here the concept is less fabulous and more imbued with earthy gusto, but it is still a powerfully original vision that rises from the stage in front, with its diagonal connections in plan and elevation and, beyond the central mass of the hay wain, loses itself in the background. The parade is organized so that despite any diversions, each detail which animates the complex is organically and completely grasped.

HIERONYMUS BOSCH. *Triptych of the Garden of Delights.*

pp. 132–133–135

This exceptional triptych is of crucial importance in correcting the usual picture of Bosch as a participant in the supernatural and the apocalyptic, in magic, alchemy and witches, in a time of bloody persecutions and trials. According to the out-moded view, in depicting enigmas and hieroglyphs, monsters and hybrids, dreamlike juxtapositions and symbols of sin and folly, Bosch is the painter of the demoniac, of obsession with sexuality and all that perturbs the religious spirit. A great mass of literary interpretations has diverted attention from Bosch's style and prevented an authentic understanding of his work. If he sometimes intentionally loaded his art with representational functions (*Christ Carrying the Cross* in Ghent, where he rivals Metsys in the adoption of Leonardo's grotesques), he based them on a rigorous and "rational" tendency to be found in Holland (Geertgen and followers, Master of the Virgo inter Virgines, etc.), and which is also connected with such French painters as Fouquet, the Master of Moulins, the Master of St. Sebastian. Furthermore, in working from the earliest Flemish masters, Bosch does not hesitate to learn from Jan van Eyck, the founding father of the tradition. There is no doubt that a fanciful intellectual climate, rich in myth and passions carried to the point of nightmare visions, gave Bosch the opportunity to insert a marvelously free kind of painting into an established idea of subject matter. The persistence of the Temptation of St. Anthony theme is better explained by the wealth of fabulous detail permitted by the legend, than by any veneration of the saint in the master's native town of 's Hertogenbosch. And his inventive faculty was undoubtedly immense, inexhaustible, to such an extent that it has favored an almost exclusive attention to his ever-surprising subject matter and reduced his work to a matter of anecdotes. The forms of his paintings, however, are not all obscure or sunk in details; their clarity is carried to a point of transparent lucidity: the "demoniac" is crystalline in every supposedly tortured image. The transformation of the real into an autonomous vision is not accomplished through an iconography of the impossible, but first of all in terms of pictorial expression. The three parts of this triptych are unified by three large concentric perspective rings (to which the terrestrial globe on the outside of the wings corresponds), while below, the rigorous distribu-

Pages 132–133–135:
HIERONYMUS BOSCH
The Garden of Delights
Triptych, in the center, *Joys of the Senses;* left, *The Garden of Eden and the Creation of Eve;* right, *Hell* (on the outside of the wings, *The Earth Created*).
Oil on panel; 7'3" × 6'5". The "painting of the variety of the world" was in the Escorial in 1593; it has been in the Prado since 1939

tion of details along diagonals (and the corresponding perspective levels) makes an extremely dense elaboration of subordinate motives possible, without dispersion or lapses in the narrative or illustration. All the individual forms are marked by a geometric purity which, in close correspondence to the rhythm, unifies each part; the part in turn is spontaneously linked with and flows into the next, with a continual transformation that is also an internal form of the highest coherency. A close rein is kept on the imaginative representation, and its reduction to basic, controlled modules. Accordingly, it is hard to know how to speak of the anxious, the troubled and the diabolic before these joyous sequences, in places somewhat ironical or frivolous, where life is seen in its infinite guises, in its hidden connections, in its possible transformations and passages, in all its impetus that pervades every creature, animate or not. Here the nature of man is exalted; it is not an orgiastic vision, but lyrically contained by a style that personalizes and harmonizes every part of the work, which is meant to be read attentively throughout its clearly marked courses, where movement and rest alternate, and everything is of equal intensity, from the choral ensemble to the most secret detail. Bosch himself may be present in the vision, in a presumed self-portrait (see upper-left detail, page 135).

HIERONYMUS BOSCH
The Garden of Delights
Four details; above left, the self-portrait of Bosch.

PIETER BREUGHEL. *The Triumph of Death.* pp. 136–137

In relation to the print *Dulle Griet,* 1564, this work may be dated between 1560 and 1566–69. The subject is derived from the Apocalypse and Ecclesiastes, but is not religious in intent or theme. It was conceived and executed for an emphatically secular reason. It is in fact connected with the massacres under the Spanish domination, and the "beggars" revolt. The work, like others, was inspired by their resistance. The oppressors, too, are snatched up by death. Companies of the dead crowd around the wagon into which a howling mob is chased by Death on horseback; even kings and cardinals are carried off in the end. There are cadavers everywhere, specters and skeletons in heaps, while in the background battles and fires rage, and on the right, gallows with their hanging burdens rise against the sky. There is no verbal equivalent for these images; in the apparent tangle, each detail is clear — a single voice in the terrible chorus. The images are locked in a composition which advances in great successive "compass turns" from the epicenter on the left toward the right, like a calculated landslide. It is reinforced by all the convergences from above and below, in an immediate and decided knot, so that there is nothing episodic in the many elements of the scene; the concentration is intense and absorbing. It is difficult to forget the scorching tragic climate that the artist has caught in this exceptional work.

Pages 136–137:
PIETER BREUGHEL
Breughel (?) ca. 1525; worked with Pieter Coecke, then in Brussels with Hieronymus Cock, engraver; Master at Antwerp in 1551; in 1552–1553 travels in Italy: Rome, Naples, Sicily; then to Antwerp; Brussels in 1563 where he died in 1569.
The Triumph of Death (ca. 1564)
Oil on panel; 3′10″ × 5′3″. Described by Karel van Mander; inventoried in San Ildefonso in 1774; at the Prado since 1827.

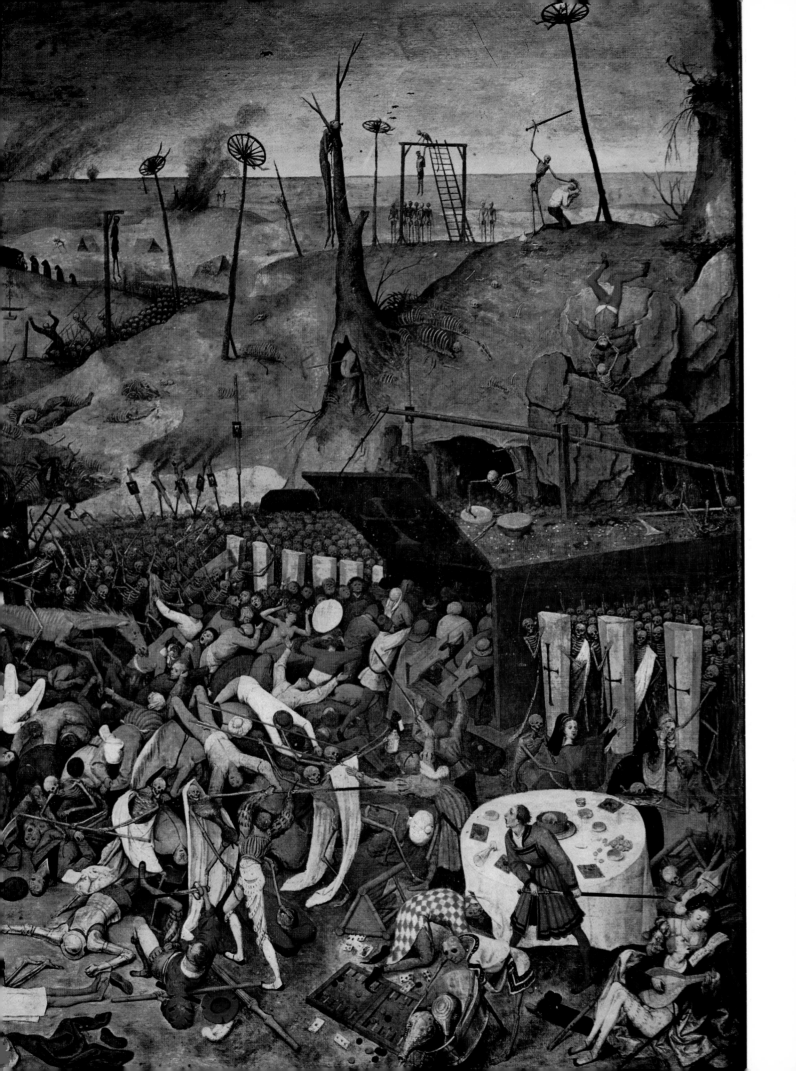

PETER PAUL RUBENS
Siegen 1577; in 1591–1598 works with
Adam van Noort and Otto van Veen; Master in 1598; in 1600 to Italy and Venice,
works in Mantua; 1601–1602 in Rome; 1603
Spain; then Mantua and Genoa; in 1608
Rome; from 1609 in Antwerp; in 1622 and
1625 in Paris; embassies to France, England and Spain in 1626–1629; in Antwerp in
1630; died there, 1640.
The Three Graces
Oil on canvas; 7'3" × 5'11 1/4". Acquired
by Philip IV from Rubens' estate; formerly
in the Royal Palace, Madrid, then in the
Academy; in the Prado since 1827.

PETER PAUL RUBENS. *The Three Graces.*

This mythology is generally dated in the last years of the artist's career, when he altered his technique by the use of oil diluted with turpentine to gain greater fluidity of tone and brushstroke. The group of the three nudes among trees (the one on the right is his wife, Hélène Fourment) is inspired by ancient models, a continual stimulus for Rubens, who was educated and nourished on classical and Italian art. But the basic theme is a celebration of physical beauty, the majestic size and brimming vitality of the three women. Their vibrant flesh is animated by the pulse of life and by the sun.

PETER PAUL RUBENS. *Diana and Her Nymphs Surprised by Fauns.*

The figures on the far left are reminiscent of Titian, who was so often interpreted by Rubens. In the last phase of his career, Rubens expressed a powerful avidity, rather than nostalgia, for life, which was reinforced by the presence of his children and of his very young wife. The pictures that he left in his estate, including this one, are almost entirely devoid of suggestions or requirements common to official commissions. They appear to have been executed to express his ardent inspiration through mythological themes, which allow in the compositional movement and in the wealth of opportunity for light and color, an agile, flowing execution, reflecting life in every motive and moment, especially in the female nudes — tremulous and warm in the moving air. The supposed collaboration of Jan Wildens in the animals and landscape does not alter the work as a whole, which is surely from Rubens' hand.

PETER PAUL RUBENS
*Diana and Her Nymphs Surprised
by Fauns*
Oil on canvas; 4'2 1/2" × 10'4".
Formerly in the Buen Retiro (1701);
since 1827 in the Prado.

PETER PAUL RUBENS. *The Judgment of Paris.* *p. 140*

Formerly listed in the palace inventories of 1666 as by Rubens, then removed from his catalogue by various scholars, the work is today again assigned to the artist and dated no later than 1605, thus belonging to his Ital-

ian period. In the classical reminiscences of the figures — though transformed by sumptuous color — Rubens composes the two groups in front of a distant Arcadian landscape. It is one of the first instances of his presenting the triumph of his feminine ideal in a Southern light: an exuberant and ardent image of his love of life.

PETER PAUL RUBENS. *Portrait of Marie de' Medici, Queen of France.*
Painted by the artist in Paris, in 1622 or 1625, this extraordinary symphony in black, white, rose and blond was executed with scorching speed. The picture was left unfinished by the artist, as seen in the exposed ocher ground and around the collar and above the head, where he kept the sketch of a trefoil solution, indicated with rapid strokes of black. From these emerges, like a flower, the head with its delicacy of tone and the very white transparent lace.

PETER PAUL RUBENS. *The Garden of Love.*   pp. 142–143
Well known through prints and replicas, this composition is at the origin of all the *conversations galantes* of the 18th century. Opposite a park with trees, there is a Roman Baroque construction with groups of statuary and fountains, while cupids hover in the air — a few are on the ground, exercising persuasion. The composition is grouped to the left; has its focus in the center and under the arch; and converges from the left with the descending figures, those at the fountain and the cupids bearing flowers. An excited and brilliant scene, teeming with incident, it is executed like a large sketch, with agile, twisting brushwork punctuated by luminous touches of opulent color. It is a hymn to joy in life. This and the other canvases of the 60-year-old Flemish master represent the inspiration that powerfully imbued his art in its final phase.

140

PETER PAUL RUBENS
The Judgment of Paris
Oil on canvas; 91″ × 114″ cm.

PETER PAUL RUBENS
*Portrait of Marie de' Medici,
Queen of France*
Oil on canvas; 4′3 1/4″ × 3′6 1/2″.
Acquired from the Rubens' estate;
in the Alcazar, Madrid (1686).

Pages 142–143:
PETER PAUL RUBENS
The Garden of Love
Oil on canvas; 6′6″ × 9′3 1/4″. Acquired from the Rubens estate; decorated Philip IV's bedroom. The canvas includes portraits of Rubens (the cavalier on the left) and his wife Hélène Fourment (center below the column).

JACOB JORDAENS. *The Artist and His Family.*

Despite the closeness to Rubens, who strongly stimulated Jordaens' style around 1621, the artist shows his independence in his choice of a powerfully sculptural form combined with energetically vehement color, which is often refined for delicate intimate effects. The composition is monumentally simple in its pyramidal center between two vertical masses. As in many other works of this period, the viewpoint is from below, to accentuate the imposing aspect of the figures and scene. In the quiet corner of the garden, light envelops the figures defined by shadows, and both the light and the shadows

JACOB JORDAENS
Antwerp 1593; with Adam van Noort in 1607; Master in 1615; Doyen in 1621; died in Antwerp, 1678.
The Artist and His Family
Oil on canvas; 5'11 1/4" × 6'3/4". The artist depicted with Catherine van Noort, whom he had married in 1616, his daughter Isabella, born 1617, and a servant. In La Granja (1746), then at Aranjuez (1794).

JACOB JORDAENS
Offerings to Ceres
Oil on canvas; 5′5″ × 3′8″.
In the inventory of the Buen
Retiro (1772).

are changeable, lighting up and dying down in a superb chromatic display.
Here a domestic scene is raised to a moment of splendor.

JACOB JORDAENS. *Offerings to Ceres.*
Earlier than the preceding work, datable around 1620, the painting is fundamental to an understanding of how Jordaens, along with the influence from Rubens, had direct recourse to Caravaggio (and not only for the dirty feet of the kneeling boy which recall the similar ones in the *Madonna of*

145

the Rosary) and acquired his sense of regular volumes and assertive solid forms that are colored and illuminated by a beam of oblique light. The "snapshot" composition (it does not appear to have been cut down), with the figures truncated and as if just coming onto the scene, and the perceptible convergence of the structure within the limited space, also are elements that come down from Caravaggio. The country people's homage to the living goddess is domestic, like the dialogue of the forms and colors, especially between the melodious greys, the warm browns and the gamut of reds, which expand in a contained symphony, dominated above by the fruit of Ceres' harvest.

ANTHONY VAN DYCK. *The Artist and Sir Endymion Porter.*

In London around 1635, the mature aristocratic art of van Dyck became more and more refined, tending toward a pervasive, sensuous taste. In this exquisite conversation portrait, two paragons of a polite and educated culture are depicted in an extremely subtle choice of colors. Their clothes are in silvery blacks and greys, while in the ocher background, dark greys and a coruscating sunset comment on the melodic song of the figures, heightening their elegance. In this period, van Dyck spiritualized his painting, which also took on nuances of ingratiating preciosity and decadence.

ANTHONY VAN DYCK. *Christ Taken Prisoner on the Mount of Olives.*

p. 148

Commissioned in 1620, this work is of Rubensian inspiration and shows the prodigious ability and extraordinary talent of the 20-year-old artist. Such mimicry did not, however, encourage the development of van Dyck's original genius, which expanded only with his visit to Italy and the consequent definition of his views and his style. In constructing the scene of the arrest, the artist (as revealed in preparatory drawings) proceeded in a crescendo of impetuosity that led to the image of the savage surprise by night and the rushing of the howling unbridled group upon the calm, serene figures of Christ and His disciples.

ANTHONY VAN DYCK
Antwerp 1599; with Henri van Baelen in 1609; Master in 1618; works with Rubens in 1620 (?); in 1621 to London, then Genoa; 1621–1623 in Genoa, Rome, Venice; 1624–1626 in Genoa, Palermo, Rome, Genoa; 1627 Antwerp; 1632 sojourn in London; in Flanders in 1634–1635 and 1640–1641; died in London, 1641.
The Artist with Sir Endymion Porter
Oil on canvas; oval, 3'10 3/4" × 4'8 1/2". Bought by Isabella Farnese in Flanders; at La Granja in 1746.
Porter, a poet, secretary of the Duke of Buckingham and art agent for Charles I, was born in Madrid in 1587, died in London, 1649.

Page 148:
ANTHONY VAN DYCK
Christ Taken Prisoner on the Mount of Olives
Oil on canvas; 11'3" × 8'2". Sketch formerly in the Cook collection (Richmond); various drawings, including one marked "Titian," which suggests a source. The work was painted for Rubens, who kept it in his house, and from whom Philip IV acquired it. In the Alcazar, Madrid (1666), then at the Buen Retiro and the New Royal Palace. Replica in Lord Methuen's collection. Corsham Court.

GERMANY
FRANCE
HOLLAND

LUCAS CRANACH
Kronach 1472 — Weimar 1553

Hunting Party in Honor of Charles V at the Castle of Torgau

Signed with initials and dated 1545. Oil on panel; 3'8 3/4" × 5'9". Its companion piece (No. 2175) is dated 1544. Replica in Lord Powerscourt's collection; other *Hunts* by Lucas and his son are in Vienna (1544), Stockholm (1546), Copenhagen and Moritzburg (1540). In the lower left are the Elector Palatine, Johann Friedrich, Duke of Saxony and the Emperor with a Knight of the Golden Fleece. Inventory of La Granja, 1746; from the collection of Isabella Farnese.

LUCAS CRANACH. *Hunting Party in Honor of Charles V at the Castle of Torgau.*

Numerous replicas and variants of this composition commemorating a deer hunt with crossbows were probably ordered by the Elector Palatine and executed by Cranach in his studio with the assistance of his sons Hans and Lucas the Younger. Cranach's early experiences were with the Danube School, with its agitation and Far Eastern exoticism, and with the humanistic ideas in Vienna and then at Martin Luther's Wittenberg. After he became Court Painter, he turned more and more to the subtle and fabulous world of the Late Gothic. He revived its nervous, undulating, broken forms, he progressively left behind Italian as well as Flemish cultural innovations. He preferred dense compositions in which to recount fables of a polite and knightly world; his taste for spectacles always included the extraordinary, the marvelous and the dramatic.

HANS BALDUNG GRIEN. *The Three Graces.*   *p. 152*

Like his other allegories of the same period (in Leipzig, Berlin, etc.) this work — datable around 1544 — represents the humanistic climate which claimed the artist, under the influence of Dürer, after the first period of his career. In the tapered figures and the harmonious composition, there are traces of a subtle linear nervousness, which Baldung also reveals in the large body of his prints. There is an open sensuousness in the female figures, vibrant and tremulous in the flow of skimming light.

ALBRECHT DÜRER. *Eve.*   *p. 153*

Certainly painted in Venice, as indicated by the epithet *Almanus* ("German"), which would not make sense in Germany, *Eve,* along with *Adam,* is of particular importance as a cultural influence. It comes at the culmination of the artist's Italian experience and reflects the ideal of proportion and harmony that will later (1528) be systematically propounded in the *Four Books of the Human Proportions,* illustrated with his drawings. Dürer openly competes with the compositional and structural standards of the Italian artists of the 15th century, as can be seen in his sculptural plasticity, in the balanced and measured correspondences of the nude elements, in the neo-antique poses (*Adam's* stance follows a Hellenic module), in the distribution of the static and dynamic balances and in the tendency toward "pure" forms within rigorously defined volumes.

The "rhetoric" does not however absorb the dancing lightness of the image between tree and branch, with its undulating hair and its body dappled by fugitive shadows.

HANS BALDUNG GRIEN
Weyersheim 1484 — with Dürer at Nuremberg in 1503–1505; in 1509 at Strasburg; 1512 at Freiburg in Breisgau; in 1517 at Strasburg, where he died in 1545.
The Three Graces
Oil on panel; 4′11 1/2″ × 2′. A companion panel represents the *Three Ages of Man and Death*. Both were given (inscription on the back of the panel) by the Count of Solms to Jean de Ligne at Frankfurt, January 23, 1547. They belonged to Philip II; in 1814 in the New Royal Palace; after the death of Ferdinand VII, in the reserves of the Prado.

ALBRECHT DÜRER
Nuremberg 1471 — with Michael Wohlgemut in 1486; journey to Colmar and Basle in 1489; in 1494 in Nuremberg, then to Venice; second sojourn in Venice 1505–1507; Flanders 1519–1520; died in Nuremberg, 1528.
Eve
Tempera on panel; 7′9″ × 2′7 1/2″. With its pendant representing *Adam,* it was given to Philip IV by Queen Christina of Sweden; in the Academy from 1777 to 1827; then in the Prado. The panel is signed and dated: *"Albertus dürer almanus/faciebat post virginis/ partum 1507* A.D."

ALBRECHT DÜRER
Portrait of a Man
Oil on panel; 19 3/4″ × 14″. Signed in
the background on the right: *"1524* A.D.*"*
Listed in Titian's "Boveda." At the
Alcazar, Madrid, in 1686.

ALBRECHT DURER
Self-Portrait
Oil on panel; 20 1/2″ × 16″. Signed under
the windowsill: *"1498/Das malt Ich nach
meiner gestalt/Ich war sex und zwanzig jor
alt/Albrecht Dürer"* ("1498/I painted this
after my form/I was twenty-six years old/
Albrecht Dürer"). In 1636, along with the
preceding portrait, it was given by the Nuremberg community to the Earl of Arundel;
acquired by Charles I; in 1686, at the Alcazar, Madrid; in the Prado from 1827.

ALBRECHT DÜRER. *Self-portrait.*

This work is also marked by Italian influence — not only Venetian but also
Raphaelesque — in the pyramid composed by the figure from the head to
the cord of the mantle and the arms with clasped hands, and in the idealiza-
tion of the figure, heroically posed, but acutely individualized. Among the
masterpieces of the artist's youth, it shows his Apollonian sentiments in an
image entirely from his own hand (which was often obliterated, even in this
early period) and marked at every point by a sensitive, subtle presence.

ALBRECHT DÜRER. *Portrait of a Man.*

Various identities have been proposed for the subject, but none is certain.
The work is from Dürer's maturity, after he had absorbed his Italian experience and returned to the intensity and the subtle explorations of his youth.
Among the paintings and drawings of this period there are a great number
of portraits, almost a pantheon of the German cultural world and Protestant
humanism.

155

NICOLAS POUSSIN. *Victorious David.*

According to Bellori, it is a work of Poussin's "first manner" and is datable around 1627. Like others belonging to this cycle, the painting is typical of the unique fusion the artist achieved through an intellectual control of his sources. At this period they were Titian and Raphael, supported by references to ancient Roman sculpture. The compositions are carefully placed in equilibrium, there is an evident framework of parallel and diagonal relationships in the linking of poses and gestures — with obvious simplifications for his particular aim of achieving formal clarity. The somewhat overdone magisterial tone is vindicated by a command of color, also programmatic, that derives from the 16th century Venetians and is expressed in sunny combinations and a springtime atmosphere, which is the fascination of this painting.

NICOLAS POUSSIN. *Landscape with Three Men.*

Datable 1645–50, when the artist adopted the classic doctrine of "modes" (heroic, tragic, pastoral, etc.), according to their literary categories, as well as the doctrine of "genres." He turned to Italian precedents for the landscape — Carracci and Domenichino — but went beyond them in an evocative and lyric invocation of the Attic spirit. As in other instances, the compositional structure is acknowledged, here built around the large ellipse linking the foreground from the stump to the tree on the left, and containing as in a bowl a many-tiered landscape that slopes toward the background crowned by clouds. Beyond its theoretical program, the landscape is imbued with a quiet atmosphere which, particularly in the "bowl" with the sheet of water to one side, determines the severe, detached quality of Poussin's vision.

NICOLAS POUSSIN
Les Andelys 1594; pupil of Varin in 1611–1612; 1612 Paris and journey to Florence; 1622 Lyons; 1624 to Rome from Venice; 1640 Paris; 1642, Rome, where he died, 1665.
Victorious David
Oil on canvas; 3'3 1/4" × 4'3 1/4". It belonged to Cardinal G. Casanate; acquired by Philip V in 1746.

NICOLAS POUSSIN
Landscape with Three Men
Oil on canvas; 3'11 1/4" × 6'1 1/2". In the
collection of Philip V, in La Granja (1746).
Another version is known. Engraved by
L. de Chatillon, ca. 1680.

CLAUDE LORRAIN. *Landscape with the Finding of Moses.*   *p. 159*
Painted around 1638, certainly by Claude's own hand, it was bought with
eight others from the artist by Philip IV. As is generally the case with his
landscapes, the figures were accessories requested by the client, and were
added by other artists to a picture which was conceived as a pure landscape.
A Frenchman in Rome, first associated with Tassi, Breenbergh and Bril,   **157**

then with Poussin, Dequesnoy, Sandrart and Pieter van Laer, Claude from his first beginnings until the years of his fame followed an independent course. He made a single-minded communion with nature — not always faithfully reproduced, in fact often interpreted fantastically — at times associated with dreams of remote, fabulous antiquity, and with scenes of palaces drenched in light, of temples, ruins and seaports lighted by the rising or the setting sun. Claude repeated this landscape, but with a different illumination between the intersecting masses of trees. Here there is a sparkling sheet of water beyond the waterfall, and beyond it extends the aqueduct towards the valley and Mount Soracte, in a haze of silvery veils under the wide sunny sky. The lyrical devotion of these landscapes as states-of-mind engrosses one in a contemplation where every consideration gives way to the root identity of man and nature. From this point of view, Claude went beyond genre in both the rustic, country-style or hunting mode and in the staging of sacred or mythological scenes — which he retained only for clients bound to literary and rhetorical themes. As an artist he opened up a new experience in history, that of the exclusive and independent choice of one's own conditions of expression. The solitary landscape, with its inviting trees and hills, with its intimate aspect of a world that can open up at any moment and at every step, is the hero of his art.

CLAUDE LORRAIN
(CLAUDE GELLÉE)
Chamagne 1600; ca. 1620 in Rome, studying with A. Tassi; in 1625 at Nancy; 1626–1627 Rome; died in Rome, 1682.
Landscape with the Findings of Moses
Oil on canvas; 6'10 1/4" × 4'6 1/4". Painted for Philip IV; No. 47 in the *Liber Veritatis*. Figures by Jacques Courtois (?). In the Buen Retiro (1701).

Page 160:
REMBRANDT VAN RIJN
Leyden 1606; in 1620, student at the university; 1620–1624 studies with Swanenburgh, Lastman, Pynas; independent from 1625; in 1632 in Amsterdam; journeys to Dordrecht, Rotterdam, The Hague in 1633; 1634–1654 in Amsterdam; in 1656 bankruptcy; 1656–1657 compulsory sales of his goods; 1661–1662 perhaps visited England; died in Amsterdam, 1669.
Sophonisbe (also called *Artemisia*)
Oil on canvas; 4'8" × 5". Signed: *"Rembrandt f. 1634."* Formerly in the Royal Palace, Madrid (1772); acquired in 1769 from the collection of the Marquesa de la Ensenada by Mengs.

REMBRANDT VAN RIJN. *Sophonisbe.* p. 160
In this work of the artist's early maturity, the basic research into light makes use of figural pretexts (silks, gold, brocades, metals, veils, jewels) to multiply the opportunities for an excited drama of light and shade and for drastically contrasted colors. But in the figure of the old woman in the background to the left there is a fabric of pure luminous touches, a synthesis of form that reduces appearances to a vibration, a sort of metaphysical beam, predicting the late masterpieces of the artist.

HISTORY OF THE MUSEUM
AND ITS BUILDING

HISTORY OF THE COLLECTIONS

The Museo del Prado in Madrid is the most important museum in Spain and one of the most notable in the world. Unquestionably it offers the richest and most complete collection of Spanish painting that exists. Of some 30,000 pictures in its possession, almost a third belongs to the Spanish school, including about 100 Goyas, about 50 of Velázquez, as many Riberas, about 20 El Grecos, and as many Zurbarans and Murillos, to mention only the most famous.

Flemish and Italian painting are also well represented at the Prado, and the story of Spanish collecting, like that in other European countries which have created museums of fundamental importance, is closely linked to the vicissitudes of the country and its political history. Spain had the fortune to be the most important European monarchy during one of the most brilliant epochs of Italian and Flemish art: the 16th century. Furthermore, those countries were in great part under the direct hegemony of Spain, and the Viceroys found themselves in the advantageous position of being able to choose among the masterpieces of those cultures to enrich the mother country. Thus, although the Prado is essentially a national gallery, in it is to be found a notable quantity of works from other lands.

*

The idea of a Spanish national gallery was born at the turn of the 18th century, stirred up in part — as in other European countries at the time — by a new interest in history and museums aroused by the Enlightenment. Yet contrary to what happened in France and England, the Spanish initiative came from the monarchy, and when the first museum was inaugurated in 1819, it was called "The Royal Museum of Painting of the Prado."

Already in 1775, the German Neo-Classic painter Anton Raffael Mengs had thought of a plan for uniting the royal collections in a museum, and in 1800 the minister Urquijo wished to create a complex for teaching the fine arts at court, including schools and museums. In 1809 a "Museo de Pinturas" was decreed, but the Napoleonic wars intervened and it was only after the restoration of King Ferdinand VII in 1814 that the arrangement of the 311 Spanish paintings was undertaken. The new museum was opened to the public five years later. It was housed in the palace of the Prado, whose construction was begun 50 years earlier under Charles III, as the seat of the Academy and Museum of the Sciences.

The entire contents of the museum at that time came from the royal collections, and the Prado grew rapidly with the addition of other works taken from palaces belonging to the crown: Palacio de la Trinidad, the Escorial and Palacio de San Ildefonso. In 1821, 195 pictures by Italian painters were added, while from 1826 to 1828 the building was enlarged and the collection increased to include 700 paintings. Ferdinand's daughter, Isabella II, tripled that figure during the 30 years of her reign, and when she went into exile in 1868, the Royal Museum became the National Museum of the Prado.

The history of the collections is tied, as has been said, to the personal taste of individual Spanish sovereigns, and to the fortunate political and economic situation of Spain in the 16th century and first half of the

17th. When Spain became a nation toward the end of the 15th century, with the union of Aragon and Castille under Ferdinand and Isabella, the taste of the court was oriented toward the painting of the Low Countries. Isabella the Catholic was a collector, but in a limited way, devoting herself exclusively to the 15th century Flemish and Dutch art, as the decoration of the royal chapel at Granada testifies. It is only with Charles V (1516–1556) that Spanish culture and taste broaden on a European scale; thus the establishment of the existing patrimony is owed to him and his enthusiasm for Italian art, which provided the royal collection with some of the Prado's splendid Titians. Charles V was the most powerful sovereign of his period in Europe and a rival of that great art patron, Francis I, King of France, who at that very time was forming the magnificent collection of works of art destined to become the foundation of the future Louvre. During his travels, Charles V was in contact with the best-known Italian artists, and one of his commissions was given to Leone and Pompeo Leoni for the magnificent bronze portrait that is now placed at the entrance to the first floor of the museum. More important, however, is the fact that he was the major and most enthusiastic patron of Titian, ordering mainly the sacred subjects he preferred, such as the *Glory* and the *Mater Dolorosa,* which entered the royal collection during his reign. Charles V's sister, Mary of Hungary, who governed the Low Countries, was also a collector, and it was she who bought the celebrated *Descent from the Cross* of Rogier van der Weyden and shipped it to Spain. Philip II (1556–1598) continued buying works by Titian and enriched the collection with such masterpieces as the *Portrait of the Artist, Danaë* and *Venus and Adonis*. His taste was more comprehensive than his father's, and he was fascinated by Bosch's eccentricities; thus he came into possession of the famous *Garden of Delights*. Works in the Prado by Sir Anthonis Mor, Luini and Jacopino del Conte go back to his reign. The collection did not grow much under Philip III (1598–1621), whose reign was distinguished by the presence in Spain of El Greco, and for the addition to the collection of Titian's *Venus Delighting in Love and Music,* which had been given to him by his relative, the Emperor Rudolph II. Philip IV (1621–1665), on the other hand, though he showed little ability as a politician, was the greatest collector Spain ever had, and the Prado's importance owes much to his initiative. He had the good fortune of being able to buy a large number of masterpieces when the very fine collection of King Charles I of England was dispersed, after Cromwell's revolution. On that occasion the royal collection acquired Mantegna's *Death of the Virgin,* Raphael's *Holy Family,* Dürer's *Self-portrait* and other pictures by Titian, Veronese and Tintoretto. Aside from these, he also acquired several paintings by Raphael and received important gifts, such as the 30 splendid Roman busts now at the Prado, the famous *Bacchanal* and the *Worship of Venus* by Titian, the *Virgin and Child and Two Saints* by Giorgione, Correggio's "*Noli Me Tangere*" and Dürer's *Eve*.

He had the wisdom to take on at court the greatest painter of the golden age of Spanish civilization, Diego Velázquez; hence the large number of paintings by his hand in the Prado, including the famous *Surrender of Breda, The Royal Family (Las Meninas), Fable of Arachne (Las Hilanderas)* and the series of court portraits. The king twice sent Velázquez to Italy to buy pictures for his collection, and the painter's purchases included Tintoretto's Old Testament scenes and Paolo Veronese's *Venus and Adonis*. Another great painter of the period, Peter Paul Rubens, was in contact with the court of Philip IV, having been there twice on diplomatic missions. The Prado is rich in his works, including the *Adoration of the Magi, The Garden of Love, The Three Graces, The Judgment of Paris* and *Perseus and Andromeda*.

Already in the reign of Philip IV, Spain had started on her decline, economically as well as politically. The decay increased under the wretched rule of Charles II (1665–1700), who had neither the means nor the intelligence to follow the great example of Philip IV. This period is remembered principally for the sojourn in Spain of the internationally famous painter, Luca Giordano, who is represented in the Prado by several works.

Isabella Farnese, the wife of Philip V (1700–1746), had her own collection, which included among other works Guido Reni's *St. Sebastian* and some notable examples of ancient sculpture; in addition, she was an enthusiastic collector of Murillo. Philip V himself bought the *Virgin and Child and Two Saints* by Giovanni Bellini, and together the royal couple made the most important acquisitions of the century when they bought the collection of the Italian painter Carlo Maratta, which included Raphael's *Holy Family under an Oak Tree* and paintings by Orazio and Artemisia Gentileschi, Albani, Castiglione and Maratta himself. Philip V was the grandson of Louis XIV of France, and the receptivity of the Spanish court to French taste is confirmed by such pictures as the *Portrait of Louis XIV* by Hyacinthe Rigaud, the *Philip and the Royal Family* by van Loo and the two canvases by Watteau at the Prado.

The accession of Charles III (1759–1788), formerly King of Naples and Sicily, aroused some interest in contemporary painting, and artists like Corrado Giaquinto, Giambattista Tiepolo and Anton Raffael Mengs came to paint at his court, in the new royal residence of Buen Retiro. At that time, the collecting of works of the past began, and the royal collection acquired a Domenichino, an Agostino Carracci and a Rembrandt. Charles IV (1788–1808) did not show a specific direction in taste when he bought Raphael's *Portrait of a Cardinal* and Metsu's *Dead Cock*. But he also bought various Spanish works, including Ribera's *Trinity,* Morales' *Presentation* and Ribalta's *St. Francis*. Undoubtedly the most important cultural event of his reign was the appearance of Francisco Goya, the most famous Spanish painter of the century. Like Velázquez more than a century earlier, he worked for the court, and the Prado possesses a splendid group of his paintings, drawings and cartoons for tapestries.

Such was the situation of the royal collections at the advent of the Napoleonic wars and the opening of the Royal Museum to the public in 1819. Ferdinand VII (1808–1833) carried on the interest in the museum, and added works of Spanish painters like Mateo Cerezo, José Antolinez and Herrera the Younger, as well as the three panels by Vicente Juan Masip and the *Trinity* by El Greco. Isabella II (1833–1868) also contributed to the museum, with acquisitions that included the celebrated *Hay Wain* by Bosch; and in that period the museum grew further with paintings taken from the royal palaces and various other residences, such as the *Annunciation* by Fra Angelico, which was discovered in a convent in 1861.

In the second half of the 19th century the museum continued to grow, with the addition of works chosen from among the thousands of pieces in the royal heritage, and in 1872 the National Museum of Painting, which formerly had been installed in the convent of the Trinitarians, became part of the Prado. This "Museo de la Trinidad" consisted of the forfeited possessions of several convents and orders that had been suppressed in 1836 and was rich in Spanish art, from El Greco to the 18th century. Other pictures came to the museum from donations, like that of Count Emil d'Erlanger (in 1881), who had bought and restored Goya's own house. In 1884 a section devoted to modern painting was opened, which was increased by a legacy of Romantic and post-Romantic paintings, the bequest of Don Ramon de Eurazan in 1904. The bequest of the Duchess of Villahermosa dates from the following year, and in 1915 Don Pablo Bosch left the museum a collection of medals and paintings.

In 1919 a restoration and enlargement of the Prado was undertaken, and in 1941 the generosity of the collector Don Francisco Cambó filled some gaps in the collection with the gift of the two Taddeo Gaddi panels, a painting by Giovanni del Ponte, the Melozzo da Forlí fresco fragment and the three scenes concerning *Nastagio degli Onesti* by Botticelli. Also during this century the museum has followed a program of increasing its holdings in Catalan primitives and foreign artists so as to represent European painting more completely, and today the Prado displays paintings by Hobbema, Salomon Koninck, Jan van Scorel, Reymerswaele, and Spanish works of the Gothic period like the *Retablo* of Don Sancho de Rojas and the group of panels by the Master of Sigüenza.

The Prado today is still primarily a gallery of paintings, but it also has a notable collection of sculpture, exhibited in the galleries along with the pictures. Most of the pieces come from the royal collection and are Greco-Roman or from the 16th to the 19th century. Among the most important objects are the San Ildefonso group of the school of Praxiteles and the stupendous Lady of Elche, an Iberian bust of the early 5th century B.C.

The Prado possesses an important collection of some 30,000 drawings, but unfortunately for reasons of space it is possible to exhibit only a small part of it, among them the masterful graphics of Goya. In addition, the museum contains furniture, ceramics, tapestries, textiles, coins and medals, coming in part from the royal collections and in part from private bequests. There is also the famous "Treasure of the Dauphin," which consists of a splendid group of chalices, gems, enamels and goldsmith work of the 16th and 17th centuries. It became the property of the Spanish crown when Philip V inherited it from his father, the Dauphin of France (eldest son of Louis XIV), and it is one of the most important of such "Treasures" in Europe.

THE BUILDING

The grandiose Palace of the Prado is the work of the architect Juan de Villanueva, of Madrid. In 1787, Charles III commissioned him to design a building for the Museum of the Sciences, and he conceived it in the form of a temple in the Neo-Classical taste. Interrupted during the Napoleonic war, the construction was resumed in 1811, after the death of the architect, and the building was assigned to house the Royal Museum.

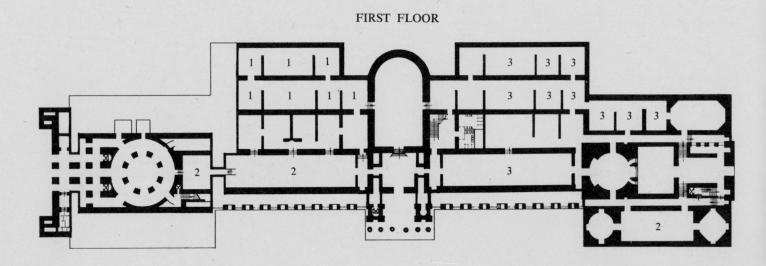

GROUND FLOOR

FIRST FLOOR

LEGEND

GROUND FLOOR
1 ITALY
2 EL GRECO
3 VELÁZQUEZ
4 FLANDERS
5 HOLLAND
6 TIEPOLO
7 ITALIAN SCHOOL 17TH CENTURY
8 FRANCE
9 GOYA
10 SPAIN
11 SPANISH PRIMITIVES
12 FLANDERS AND
   GERMANIC COUNTRIES

FIRST FLOOR
1 GOYA
2 SPAIN 16TH–17TH CENTURIES
3 SPAIN, FLANDERS,
   HOLLAND 17TH–18TH CENTURIES

SECOND FLOOR
1 FRANCE 17TH–18TH CENTURIES
2 FERNANDEZ-DURAN BEQUEST
3 FLANDERS 17TH–18TH CENTURIES
4 ITALY 16TH–17TH CENTURIES
5 SPAIN 17TH–18TH–19TH CENTURIES

BASEMENT
1 VARIOUS SCHOOLS
2 ENGLISH PORTRAIT
   PAINTERS 18TH–19TH CENTURIES

SECOND FLOOR

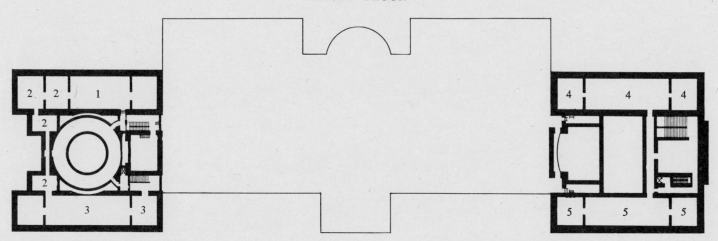

BASEMENT

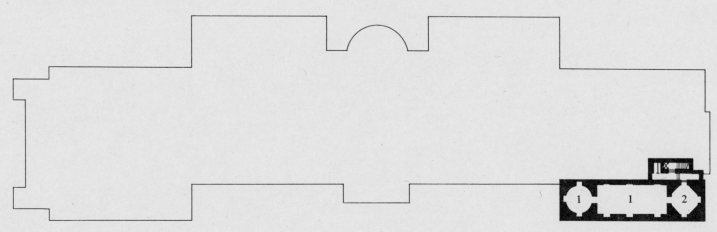

SELECTED BIBLIOGRAPHY

A. L. MAYER. *Francisco de Goya*. London and Toronto, 1924.

C. R. POST. *A History of Spanish Painting* (14 vols.). Cambridge, Mass., 1930 — (Vol. XIV, 1966).

Museo del Prado, *Catalogo*. Madrid, 1933.

MARIANO DE MADRAZO. *Historia del Museo del Prado*. Madrid, 1945.

J. CAMÓN AZNAR. *Domonico Greco* (2 vols.). Madrid, 1950.

F. J. SÁNCHEZ CANTÓN. *Vida y Obras de Goya*. Madrid, 1951.

JACQUES LASSAIGNE. *Spanish Painting: From the Catalan Frescos to El Greco; Spanish Painting: From Velázquez to Picasso*. New York, 1952.

Los Dibujos de Goya del Museo del Prado. Madrid, 1952.

GIAN ALBERTO DELL'ACQUA. *Tiziano*. Milan, 1955.

ASENJO BLANCO. *Catalogo de la Escultura*. Madrid, 1957.

HAROLD E. WETHEY. *El Greco and His School* (2 vols.). Princeton, 1962.

HARRY B. WEHLE. *Great Paintings from the Prado Museum*. New York, 1963.

JOSÉ LÓPEZ-REY. *Velázquez; A Catalogue Raisonné of his Oeuvre*. London, 1963.

Museo del Prado, *Catalogo de las Pinturas*. Madrid, 1963.

INDEX OF ILLUSTRATIONS

169

INDEX OF NAMES

171

GENERAL INDEX